POPULAR
MUSIC

The Popular Music Series

Popular Music, 1980–1989, is a revised cumulation of and supersedes Volumes 9 through 14 of the *Popular Music* series, all of which are still available:

Volume 9, 1980–84	Volume 10, 1985
Volume 11, 1986	Volume 12, 1987
Volume 13, 1988	Volume 14, 1989

Popular Music, 1920–1979, is a revised cumulation of and supersedes Volumes 1 through 8 of the *Popular Music* series, of which Volumes 6 through 8 are still available:

Volume 1, 2nd ed., 1950–59	Volume 2, 1940–49
Volume 3, 1960–64	Volume 4, 1930–39
Volume 5, 1920–29	Volume 6, 1965–69
Volume 7, 1970–74	Volume 8, 1975–79

Popular Music, 1900–1919, is a companion volume to the revised cumulation.

This series continues with:

Volume 15, 1990	Volume 16, 1991
Volume 17, 1992	Volume 18, 1993
Volume 19, 1994	Volume 20, 1995
Volume 21, 1996	Volume 22, 1997
Volume 23, 1998	Volume 24, 1999
Volume 25, 2000	Volume 26, 2001

Other Books by Gary Graff

MusicHound Country: The Essential Album Guide

MusicHound Folk: The Essential Album Guide

MusicHound Jazz: The Essential Album Guide

MusicHound Lounge: The Essential Album Guide

MusicHound R&B: The Essential Album Guide

MusicHound Rock: The Essential Album Guide

ISSN 0886-442X

VOLUME 27
2002

POPULAR MUSIC

An Annotated Guide to American Popular Songs,
Including Introductory Essay, Lyricists & Composers Index,
Important Performances Index,
Awards Index, and List of Publishers

GARY GRAFF
Editor

MICHAEL T. READE
Project Editor

GALE®

Detroit • New York • San Diego • San Francisco • Cleveland
New Haven, Conn. • Waterville, Maine • London • Munich

Popular Music, Volume 27

Gary Graff, Editor

Project Editor
Michael T. Reade

Editorial
Andrew C. Claps

Editorial Systems Support
Charles Beaumont, Venus Little

Product Design
Kate Scheible, Tracey Rowens

Composition and Electronic Prepress
Evi Seoud

Manufacturing
Stacy Melson

LIBRARY OF CONGRESS CATALOG CARD NUMBER 85-653754

ISBN 0-7876-7221-1
ISSN 0886-442X

Contents

Introduction

This volume is the twenty-seventh in a series whose aim is to set down in permanent and practical form a selective, annotated list of the significant popular songs of our times. Other indexes of popular music have either dealt with special areas, such as jazz or theater and film music, or been concerned chiefly with songs that achieved a degree of popularity as measured by the music-business trade indicators, which vary widely in reliability.

Annual Publication Schedule

The first nine volumes in the *Popular Music* series covered sixty-five years of song history in increments of five or ten years. With Volume 10, a new, annual publication schedule was initiated, making background information available as soon as possible after a song achieves prominence. Yearly publication also allows deeper coverage—approximately five hundred songs—with additional details about writers' inspirations, uses of songs, album appearances, and more.

Indexes

Three indexes make the valuable information in the song listings even more accessible to users. The Lyricists & Composers Index shows all the songs represented in *Popular Music, Volume 27*, that are credited to a given individual. The Important Performances Index tells at a glance which albums, musicals, films, television shows, or other media are represented in the volume. The "Performer" category—first added to the index as "Vocalist" in Volume 11—allows the user to see which songs an artist has been associated with this year. The index is arranged by broad media category, then alphabetically by show or album title, with the songs listed under each title. Finally, the Awards Index provides a list of songs nominated for awards by the American Academy of Motion Picture Arts and Sciences (Academy Award) and the American Academy of Recording Arts and Sciences (Grammy Award). Winning songs are indicated by asterisks.

List of Publishers

The List of Publishers is an alphabetically arranged directory that provides addresses—when available—for the publishers of songs represented in *Popular Music, Volume 27*. Also noted is the organization that handles performance rights for the particular publisher: in the United States, the American Society of Composers, Authors, and

Publishers (ASCAP) or Broadcast Music, Inc. (BMI); in Canada, the Society of Composers, Authors, and Music Publishers of Canada (SOCAN); and in Europe, the Society of European Songwriters and Composers (SESAC).

Acquiring Song Information

Unfortunately, the basic records kept by the active participants in the music business are often casual, inaccurate, and transitory. There is no single source of comprehensive information about popular songs, and those sources that do exist do not offer complete information about even the musical works with which they are directly concerned. Four of the primary proprietors of basic information about popular music are the major performing-rights societies: ASCAP, BMI, SOCAN, and SESAC. Although these organizations have considerable information about the songs of their own writer and publisher members, their electronic files are designed primarily for clearance identification by commercial users of music. The files, while extensive in scope, are not necessarily exhaustive, and the facts given about the songs are also limited. ASCAP, BMI, SOCAN, and SESAC are, however, invaluable and indispensable sources of data about popular music.

Another basic source of information about musical compositions and their creators and publishers is the Copyright Office of the Library of Congress. A computerized file lists each published, unpublished, republished, and renewed copyright of songs registered with the Office. There is a time lag (typically a number of months) from the time of application until songs are officially registered (in some cases, songs have already been released before copyright registration begins). This file is helpful in determining the precise date of the declaration of original ownership of musical works, but since some authors, composers, and publishers have been known to employ rather makeshift methods of protecting their works legally, there are songs listed in *Popular Music* that might not be found in the Library of Congress files.

Selection Criteria

In preparing the original volumes for this time period, the staff was faced with a number of separate problems. The first and most important of these was that of selection. The stated aim of the project—to offer the user as comprehensive and accurate a listing of significant popular songs as possible—has been the guiding criterion. The purpose has never been to offer a judgment on the quality of any songs or to indulge a prejudice for or against any type of popular music. Rather, it is the purpose of *Popular Music* to document those musical works that (a) achieved a substantial degree of popular acceptance; (b) were exposed to the public in especially notable circumstances; or (c) were accepted and given important performances by influential musical and dramatic artists.

Another problem was whether or not to classify the songs as to type. Most works of music are subject to any number of interpretations, and although it is possible to describe a particular performance, it is more difficult to give a musical composition a label applicable not only to its origin but also to its subsequent musical history. In fact, the most significant versions of some songs are often quite at variance with the songs' origins. Citations for such songs in *Popular Music* indicate the important facts about not only the songs' origins but also their subsequent lives, rather than assigning an arbitrary and possibly misleading label.

Research Sources

The principal sources of information for the titles, authors, composers, publishers, and dates of copyright of the songs in this volume were ASCAP, BMI, SOCAN, SESAC, the Copyright Office of the Library of Congress, and album notes. For historical notes; information about foreign, folk, public domain, and classical origins; and identification of theatrical, film, and television introducers of songs, the staff relied upon *Billboard* magazine, album notes, Web sites such as All Music Guide (http://www.allmusic.com), CDNOW (http://www.cdnow.com), Rock on the Net (http://www.rockonthenet.com), and other materials.

Acknowledgments

The preparers of *Popular Music, Volume 27*, would like to thank Daniel Durchholz for researching and compiling the performance and publication data used in this book.

User's Guide

Contents of a Typical Entry

The primary listing for a song includes

❙1❙ title
❙2❙ author(s) and composer(s)
❙3❙ current publishers, copyright date
❙4❙ annotation on the song's origins or performance history

Description of Numbered Elements

❙1❙ Title. The full title—and, when appropriate, alternate title—is given as it appears in the preponderance of the source material. Since even a casual perusal of the book reveals considerable variation in spelling and punctuation, it should be noted that these are the colloquialisms of the music trade and that every effort has been made to capture the most reliable and accurate data possible.

❙2❙ Authorship. In all cases, the primary listing reports the author(s) and composer(s). The reader may find variations in the spelling of a songwriter's name. This results from the fact that some writers used different forms of their names at different times or in connection with different songs. In addition to this kind of variation in the spelling of writers' names, the reader will also notice that in some cases, where the writer is also the performer, the name as writer may differ from the form of the name used as performer.

❙3❙ Publisher. The current publisher or publishers are listed. Since *Popular Music* is designed as a practical reference work rather than an academic study, and since copyrights more than occasionally change hands, the current publisher is given instead of the original copyright holder.

❙4❙ Annotation. The primary listing mentions significant details about the song's history, including performer; album, film, or other production in which the song was introduced or featured; any other performers appearing on the song; record company; awards; and other relevant data. The name of a performer may be listed differently in connection with different songs, especially over a period of years. The name listed is the form of the name given in connection with a particular performance or record. Dates are provided for important recordings and performances.

Popular Music in 2002

The world of music was not without things to celebrate in 2002.

As the specter of the September 11 terrorist attacks began to diminish and life returned to a degree of normalcy, there were signs of great creative and aesthetic health. Rappers Eminem and Nelly delivered blockbuster successes—the former prevailing in both the music stores and in the movie theaters. Canadian teen rocker Avril Lavigne was a fresh-faced, mutli-platinum newcomer who provided a growth bridge for pop fans once infatuated with *NSYNC, the Backstreet Boys and Britney Spears, while Norah Jones brought a new level of sophistication into the Top 40.

The Dixie Chicks emerged from legal loggerheads with its record company to produce the most ambitious album of their career, and Bruce Springsteen's *The Rising* took 9/11 from conceptual to human terms. Shania Twain returned to the scene as Garth Brooks was exiting. Wily veterans such as Paul McCartney and the Rolling Stones scored big at the concert box offices, while a wave of new garage rockers stripped the music back to its basics.

And an America enamored of reality TV shows let music enter that mix with the "Star Search" meets "Survivor" appeal of "American Idol."

But in 2002, all of these successes were merely the silver lining of an extremely dark and ominous cloud. The music industry, at least as we know it, was in deep trouble, with no sure sign of how it was going to combat it.

Sales were down again in 2002—a hefty and panic-inducing 10 percent from previous years. The industry was quick to blame the decline on Internet file sharing, increased CD burning and more competition (video games, movies, a booming DVD market and, again, the Internet) for the entertainment dollar. A flagging economy certainly contributed, too. Consumers largely agreed, but pointed out that were it not for too-high CD prices, they might not be copying or stealing the music in the first place.

The industry responded with layoffs—of employees and artists—mergers and other cost-cutting measures. It didn't make any significant moves to lower CD prices, but it did initiate enhancements such as bonus video material and CD-triggered exclusive Internet sites that offered consumers a slew of extra features. And even as they stepped up combative measures against the on-line file sharing services such as Kazaa, Morpheus and Grokster—including litigation and legislative lobbying—executives did make vague noises about trying to cut CD prices in the near future.

Still, the impression was left throughout the industry that record companies, and particularly the major labels, were losing the ability to effectively distribute and promote music, which in turn left artists contemplating a future that would be more self-contained and self-directed.

The concert industry also faced troublesome signs during the year. Certain numbers were encouraging; all-time highs for total attendance (42 million) and ticket sale grosses ($1.7 billion). But those masked declines in average per-show attendance (down 10.6 percent) and per-show grosses (down 8.5 percent), meaning that higher ticket prices and a greater number of concerts mitigated losses that did not bode well for the health of that sector of the business, either.

The signs, then, made it clear that the music industry was teetering on a fault line that could put its very existence in jeopardy. No wonder, then, that it was far more comforting to avert our eyes—and ears—to pay attention to the state of the music itself.

Eminem Shows

The real Slim Shady stood up tall in 2002. Eminem continued his phenomenal rise with a trio of high-profile triumphs—his third album, *The Eminem Show*, a headlining slot on the year's Anger Management tour and his first feature film, "8 Mile," for which the rapper scored an MTV Movie Award for Best Male Actor and an Academy Award for the song "Lose Yourself."

The Eminem Show came first, in the spring, and led by the good-humored single "Without Me," it sold 7.4 million copies—making it the top-selling album of the year. It also brought forth an Eminem who, while still angry, offered a broader vision and palate of topics, openly addressing the politics of Washington, D.C., as well as the politics of success as a white rapper.

"There's always gonna be things to talk about—What goes on in my personal life, what goes on in the world, whatever happens," Eminem told the BBC. "I just talk about everything in this record."

But if an Eminem record can be overshadowed by anything else in his life, "8 Mile" was it.

Arriving in theaters on a tidal wave of hype, the Curtis Hanson-directed movie—which was filmed in his native Detroit—told the story of an aspiring white rapper in Detroit beset with family problems and credibility issues within the rap community. Sporting a genuinely dynamic performance by Eminem, particularly during the galvanizing rap battle scenes, "8 Mile" was a box office success accompanied by a soundtrack whose sales—3.2 million copies—put it at fifth-place on the year-end list. In early November he also had a hat trick of the No. 1 movie, album (*Music From and Inspired by...8 Mile*) and song ("Lose Yourself") in the country.

"Honestly, when it was in the works, we weren't even talking about making it that big of a project," Eminem said. "We had no idea it was gonna do what it did—otherwise we would've asked for more goddamn money!"

But while "8 Mile" clearly drew on elements of his past, Eminem took great pains to distance himself from the tale.

"It wasn't a story about my life," he contended. "It could've been anybody's story, really. I wanted to basically show it from my side of the tracks. There's so many people that grew up and are growing up like I grew up. I just wanted to make a movie that felt it was real and true to my heart."

Eminem was without peer as 2002's artist of the year, but his runner-up was another rapper—St. Louis's Nelly, whose sophomore effort, *Nellyville*, sold 4.8 million copies and launched the sexy party anthem "Hot in Herre" as well as "Dilemma," his duet with Destiny's Child's Kelly Rowland that appeared both on *Nellyville* and on her solo debut, *Simply Deep*. Nelly was also an in-demand guest in 2002, with his most striking cameo on the Neptunes' remix of *NSYNC's "Girlfriend."

Girls, Girls, Girls

Also stealing a spotlight in 2002 was Avril Lavigne, an 18-year-old rocker from tiny Napanee, Ontario (population 5,000), whose first album, *Let's Go*, sold more than 13 million copies worldwide and launched new pop and modern rock anthems such as "Complicated" and "Sk8er Boi;" the former, in fact, set record when it logged 16 consecutive weeks at No. 1 on the Nielsen SoundScan Adult Top 40 charts.

Lavigne was nominated for five Grammy Awards (she walked away empty-handed) and won four Juno Awards in her native Canada. "Complicated" was nominated for the prestigious Ivor Novello Award, a British honor for songwriting. And Lavigne was named the Most Sexy Woman in music at this year's Brit Awards—though unlike contemporaries such as Britney Spears, Christina Aguilera and Pink, Lavigne prefers more modest attire such as jeans, T-shirts, rubber bracelets and, at one point, men's ties, and eschews gratuitous displays of skin.

"That's not what I'm gonna do," noted Lavigne, whose tomboyish upbringing included plenty of hockey, skateboarding and camping. "I don't need to show the world my booty, my belly or my boobs—and I have a great body! But I'm selling my music, not my body."

Still, Lavigne acknowledged that she was overwhelmed by her success which crossed over a variety of formats and brought guitar-oriented sounds back to pop scene that had been dominated by vocal groups and midriff-baring divas.

"I don't think anyone really thought it would do this well," she explained. "Didn't think about how well it would do—didn't know what I thought or expected. I just knew I wanted to do this with my life and always believed in myself."

Three other female singer-songwriters made believers out of the pop world in 2002 as well.

Norah Jones, the daughter of Indian sitar virtuoso Ravi Shankar, dazzled listeners with *Come Away With Me*, a debut album that mixed country, western and jazz influences with jazz and pop stylings for sound that was both retro and fresh. "Don't Know Why" was the big hit, and Jones' seven-times platinum triumph would wind up nabbing five trophies at the 2003 Grammy Awards.

Arizona teenager Michelle Branch rode the momentum started by her 2001 title "Everywhere," launching more hits such as "Goodbye to You" and "All You Wanted" as her debut album, *The Spirit Room*, went platinum.

Branch also had the honor of being tapped to guest on "The Game of Love," first single from the Santana album *Shaman*. "She's a very special soul," Carlos Santana noted. "I feel really inspired being around her. For being such a young person, she's an old soul. She has the qualities to be around for a long time."

Branch, meanwhile, found all of this "unexpected," especially since she felt her straightforward brand of melodic rock was "not really pop enough to be pop and not really rock enough to be rock."

"I just kind of walked into this and said, 'Hey, I'm just doing what I'm doing,'" Branch explained. "The stuff I'm doing isn't really on pop radio or anything. I just said, 'You know what? I'm just gonna see what happens when I get there.'"

2002's quartet of hot female newcomers was rounded out by Vanessa Carlton, a piano-playing singer-songwriter—and Columbia University student—whose debut album, *Be Not Nobody*, made her somebody thanks to the hit "A Thousand Miles." During a summer tour with the Goo Goo Dolls and Third Eye Blind, Carlton also snagged a boyfriend—3EB frontman Stephan Jenkins—though she was loathe to spend too much time talking about it.

"We are together, but it's not something that I'd like to make public or kind of capitalize on; it's not like a [Jennifer Lopez] and Ben [Affleck] thing or anything like that," Carlton said. "It's so strange; suddenly you're in the public eye, and I'm such a private person. I mean, I wouldn't tell a stranger who I'm dating, and I wouldn't talk to them about my love life."

Idol Worship

America developed a new musical love affair during 2002—"American Idol." The Fox Network TV show, based on a British program called "Pop Idol," featured performances from contestants culled from more than 10,000 hopefuls. The finalists were systemically pared down via viewer votes until just one—bubbly, big-voiced Texan Kelly Clarkson—was chosen THE American Idol in a final broadcast that was watched by 23 million people.

Clarkson's reward; a recording contract that started with the single "A Moment Like This," which set a new Billboard chart record by jumping from No. 52 to No. 1—the last leap ever—with first-week sales of 236,000 copies. And *American Idol: Great Moments*, an album featuring performances by the 10 finalists, debuted at No. 4 the Billboard album chart.

A follow-up TV special, "American Idol in Vegas," was another ratings bonanza, and a concert tour by the 10 finalists sold out in record time across the country.

Clarkson was as surprised as anyone that "Idol" became as popular as it did. Her try; a mix of compelling personalities—not only the contestants but also cutie-pie hosts Ryan Seacrest and Brian Dunkelman and acerbic judge Simon Cowell (who served on a panel with Paula Abdul and Randy Jackson)—and the fact that the audiences able to vote for the winners set "Idol" apart from predecessors such as "Star Search" or "Making the Band."

"People were tired of watching shows where people just got put together or something," Clarkson said. "This time they had a say. They got to choose who they thought should win or advance, and that made them care more."

Clarkson was hardly the only "Idol" winner, however. Runner-up Justin Guarini landed a recording contract as well, and both were slotted to star in a beach-party music "From Justin to Kelly," for the summer of 2003.

"I think from the very beginning, once we found out 'Wow, this is what it is?', we realized it doesn't matter whether we finish 10th or first," Guarini said. "It was a great opportunity no matter what. We've had experience, exposure, learned lessons you can't pay for."

And the music industry learned a new way to create and market hits.

"A record company is generally trying to create demand for an artist, but in this case, there's plenty of demand out there already," said Aaron Borns of RCA Records, which signed Clarkson. "It's a lot of fun. It's different for us and for the audience."

A Bit More Girl Power

Ashanti was not a stranger when she released her self-titled debut album in 2002. The former dancer and actress ("Malcolm X," "Who's da Man?"), discovered by Murder Inc. chief Irv Gotti, was set up with hit duets with Ja Rule ("Always on Time") and Fat Joe ("What's Luv?"); the arrival of her own single, "Foolish," gave her three Top 10 hits in the same week, pumping the *Ashanti* album to sales of more than half a million copies in its first week (it went on to sell more than three million copies). With subsequent singles such as "Baby" and "Happy," and a grafted-on duet with the late Notorious B.I.G. on "Unfoolish," Ashanti was perhaps the year's most ubiquitous presence.

So was singer/actress Jennifer Lopez, who joined Eminem in having a No. 1 album (*This is Me...Then*) at the same time she had the top-grossing film ("Maid in New York"). Lopez followed Ashanti's duet strategy as well, joining forces with rappers 50 Cent ("I'm Gonna Be Alright"), Ja Rule ("Ain't it Funny") and Jadakiss and Styles ("Jenny From the Block").

Pink may have gotten the party started for her second album, *M!ssundaztood*, in 2001, but the festivities raged well into 2002. She sold another three million copies of the album, thanks to subsequent singles such as "Don't Let Met Get Me," "You Make Me Sick" and "Just Like a Pill."

It was a good year for Sheryl Crow, too. Her fifth album, *c'mon, c'mon*, was propelled to No. 2 on the charts thanks to the buoyant first single "Soak Up the Sun." It was her first set of original material since 1998's *The Globe Sessions*, and emerged after a bit of writer's block and a break-up with actor Owen Wilson.

But for Crow, the triumph was making it to 40 (she turned 41 in 2002) and not only still having a hot enough body to show off in her CD booklet photos but also to still be a potent force in the pop market.

"I think there's expectations of turning 40," she said. "I think 40 represents, historically, the endings of things and the beginning of things. The ending of your child-bearing years, for instance. And certainly in this business it represents not being the young, hip kid anymore. It's the beginning of slowing down, the beginning of the downhill slope of your art or whatever."

Shania Twain also returned to the scene after a long break; her *Up!* came five years after *Come on Over*, which was 18 times platinum. *Up!* definitely headed in that direction, selling 2.6 million copies in just over a month of release and is looking toward keeping the momentum going into 2003.

Not so powerful in 2002 was "The Ketchup Song (Hey Hah)" by the female vocal trio Las Ketchup. It did enjoy success in the dance clubs, but those hoping and/or expecting it to be another "Macarena" were sorely disappointed.

Sobering Expressions

The horrors of September 11 were not forgotten in 2002; in fact, while 2001 saw the embrace of "songs of healing"—including Nickelback's "How You Remind Me" (which was also the most-played song of 2002) and Five For Fighting's "Superman (It's Not Easy)"—the year saw artists produce a substantial body of musical work that evolved from reactions to the events to reflections on the aftermath that sometimes openly question the actions taken by government and society in their wake.

"This is what an artist, a songwriter, is supposed to do," explained rock veteran Graham Nash. "I've always tried to get up in the morning...and get on with my day and write about what affects me and what pisses me off and what I laugh about and what I fall in love with."

Added New York-based jazz musician Leni Stern—who wrote the song "Where is God?" after September 11—"Us storytellers are supposed to tell a story about something and heal the wounds, to help people go through troubled times and keep a sense of hope and a sense of themselves."

Even musicians who don't consider themselves "political" acknowledge some influence from those events.

"I guess when I write, I write about things I experience myself," said Sully Erna of the Boston hard rock band Godsmack. "I may not write specifically about 9-11, but it becomes part of the fabric of my emotions, you know?"

The musical responses to September 11 have cut a broad emotional swath via both individual songs and full-length works—of which Bruce Springsteen's *The Rising* was the most successful artistically and commercially. Yet he was far from alone.

Neil Young appropriated the words of United Airlines Flight 93 passenger Todd Beamer for "Let's Roll," his salute to the passengers on that flight who attacked the terrorist hijackers who were reportedly trying to crash the plane in Washington. Paul McCartney, who was on an airport runway in Newark, N.J., at the time of the attacks, quickly penned his ode to "Freedom" and performed it at the 2002 Super Bowl.

Country singer Alan Jackson adopted a mournful tone for "Where Were You (When the World Stopped Turning)?", with its common-man sentiment of not knowing the difference between Iran and Iraq; he debuted the song at the Country Music Awards in November of 2001 and then released it on his *Drive* album in 2002. Meanwhile, fellow Nashvillian Toby Keith sounded a defiant "don't tread on me" battle cry with his hit "Courtesy Of The Red, White And Blue (The Angry American)"—which ABC deemed too strident for Keith to perform on its special July 4 broadcast.

And the performance art troupe Blue Man Group created a sober, moving video titled "Exhibit 13" that was inspired by the rain of papers and debris from the World Trade Center that blew over New York's East River and into Brooklyn.

Sheryl Crow found that "Safe and Sound," a song she wrote pre-9/11 about what she felt was the Bush administration's disregard for the environment, "ended up taking on a new shape" after she performed it during the "America: A Tribute to Heroes" telethon. Ditto for Creed's earnest paean "My Sacrifice," which was written in the spring of 2001 for the group's *Weathered* album, which was released that November.

"That...freaked us out," says Creed frontman Scott Stapp. "We attribute it to just being in tune with the world, and maybe after September 11 people interpreted some of those songs as being a reflection of the state of their minds and how they felt."

While the public was embracing those songs, however, more specific material was in the creative pipeline. Jackson wrote "Where Were You..." during a sleepless night in October; Young canonized Beamer and the other Flight 93 passengers because he felt their action "was so heroic it just had to be captured." Springsteen, meanwhile, wrote songs for *The Rising* at his farm home in Monmouth County, the New Jersey area hit hardest by the tragedy; some of the tracks were informed by conversations he had with spouses of the attack victims.

Springsteen's New Jersey neighbor Jon Bon Jovi and his band, meanwhile, drew inspiration for several songs from its 2002 album *Bounce* from the aftermath of the tragedy—though he notes that it wasn't easy.

"We worked until we could find a voice that I felt was right-on and I could speak from truthfully and honestly and not with any fiction involved," explained Bon Jovi. "I couldn't put myself in the shoes of the widower; I wasn't the widower. I knew the widower, but I didn't sleep in his head at night. I knew how I felt, so I could write 'Everyday.' I knew what my community was going through, so I could write 'Bounce' and 'Undivided.'

"But I didn't want to release the [songs] that we were writing which were kind of 'I'm waiting for you to come home,' 'How could this have happened us?', those kinds of things, because I didn't live them first-hand. My community did. My friends did. But my family was safe."

The attacks also spurred Tori Amos to work in earnest on a broad, expansive work called, *Scarlet's Walk*, which she called "an aural journey of America" that treats the country itself as a living entity.

"We were out on the road at a time when a lot of people were canceling" in the fall of 2001, Amos recalled. "People were seeming to look at 'America' not as an object but as a being, almost, a friend—'What about *her,* she who is our land?' That kind of thing.

"This is nothing new to other cultures, but to America, it was."

And Emily Saliers of the Indigo Girls, which had just started recording its latest album, added new lyrics to her song "Our Deliverance" "about soldiers and war and how violence begats violence"—a potentially daring sentiment at a time when the popular sentiment ran in favor of vengeance and military action.

But as time went on, more songwriters detached themselves from the emotions of September 11 and dealt with other aspects that surfaced in its wake. Heavy metal singer Ronnie James Dio, for instance, wrote "Rock & Roll" after hearing about the ClearChannel Communications radio conglomerate's list of songs it recommended stations not play after the attacks.

"I thought it was just absolutely criminal for them to just blindly take songs they thought might have an offensive title or something they felt directly correlated to the tragedy," Dio says. "To me, it was just the ultimate form of censorship and the most *un*-American thing I could think of."

Neil Young called the ClearChannel list "the stupidest thing I've ever heard of. [Simon & Garfunkel's] 'Bridge Over Troubled Water' is on the list—what the hell's wrong with *that* song?"

The Chicago hard rock band Disturbed, meanwhile, was so, well, disturbed by comments made by conservative commentators Jerry Falwell and Pat Buchanan about how American society's loose morals brought the attacks upon it that it responded with "Prayer" for the group's second album *Believe*.

"I was incensed by [their comments]," said frontman Dave Dramian. "I think what really frightens me about the situation is how everyone has used it as a means of empowering themselves or taking away freedoms.

"I couldn't believe this idea that there's too much homosexuality and abortion and promiscuity and we were being punished for it—and, oh, by the way, we can save your soul for a measly contribution of X dollars to the church."

The greatest firestorm, however, was generated by "John Walker's Blues," from Nashville singer-songwriter Steve Earle's album *Jerusalem*. The song was inspired by the story of John Walker Lindh, the American youth who adopted Islam and took up with the Taliban. Earle did not defend Lindh—"I feel urgently American," he said—but he did draw a sympathetic picture of someone he feels was treated with undue harshness.

"Nobody accused John Walker Lindh of shooting anyone or blowing anything up," explained Earle, who was castigated by conservative commentators when the song's lyrics leaked out in August. "He's not guilty of *treason;* he's just this kid who got himself into Islam and wound up in Afghanistan. I believed a lot of stuff when I was 20, too...

"But it quickly became apparent that [the U.S. government] was gonna do this kid 'cause they couldn't catch Osama [Bin Laden]. I just felt like what happened to him was so quiet and behind closed doors, especially considering it was in our civilian court system...Our willingness to impale our civil liberties on our fear scared me."

The impact of September 11 on music will likely continue for years as artists seek perspective on the event—and comment on its continuing effects, such as the U.S.-led war on terrorism and looming military action against Iraq. Melissa Etheridge, for instance, said her next album would include a song that's "not so much about 9-11 as it is about our choices as a country since then."

And we can probably expect some, if not much, of what's coming to swerve a bit from a strict red, white and blue dogma.

"I feel like I'm a patriot; I totally love America and support my country," said Everclear's Art Alexakis. "But at the same time I believe that to be a patriot and to be someone who believes in America and the American way of life does not mean wrapping yourself in the flag and pulling it over your head.

"It's our right and our duty to question authority when we believe it oversteps its bounds. Too many people are trying to push it to this place of 'How dare you question the president!' That's my job, man. That's everybody's job."

Home Is Where the Heart Is

The Dixie Chicks' third album, *Home*, was one of the most heartening triumphs of 2002. The Texas trio's unexpectedly unadorned and rootsy affair was a marked change from the glossy pop-country of its multi-platinum predecessors, yet it still managed to debut at No. 1 its first week out and notch sales of more than three million copies after just a few weeks.

But even though it sounded different, the group's Emily Robison said that "we feel it's some of our more pop or crossover [music], in the broadest sense of the term."

Home had its start literally in the group members' living rooms, where they were working up new songs while embroiled in a battle with their label, Sony Music, over their royalty rate and other conditions of their contract. The trio declared itself a free agent and even began talking to other labels, starting a series of lawsuits and countersuits that was ultimately settled with the Chicks establishing their own Sony-distributed imprint, Wide Open Records.

All was well that ended well, but Robison acknowledged that it was a "frustrating" time at best. And frightening. "It's a scary thing when you step out like that and go 'OK, with this record label we've sold 21 million albums, and here we are saying we're labelless,'" she explained. "Who's gonna pick up the pieces and put this thing back together, y'know? Luckily we came to an agreement with Sony and they stepped up and did the right thing, and we are where we are."

The tumult, however, helped bring the group back to a more simple musical approach, one that recalled the sound Robison and her sister, Marti Maguire, pursued when they started the band in 1989 as a kitschy cowgirl bluegrass outfit.

"We come from bluegrass and acoustic music," said Robison. "It was natural to play this way. It was nice to be back in the studio where you knew your part wasn't necessarily going to be buried amongst drums and keyboards and all that sort of stuff, knowing it was gonna be fairly raw.

"Once we started playing it for our management and people whose opinions we really value, they were like 'Y'all would be crazy not to have this be the third album.'"

Boy Oh Boys

In 2002's pop music market, boys still wanted to be boys—but not necessarily in boy bands.

The youngest members of both *NSYNC and Backstreet Boys—Justin Timberlake and Nick Carter, respectively—decided to go solo. Both earnestly claimed they were still part of their groups but that they both wanted to "grow" and "explore" other areas of music. Timberlake's more successful *Justified* took the pop/R&B blend of *NSYNC in edgier directions—with one ballad, "Cry Me a River," that addressed his breakup with girlfriend and fellow pop star Britney Spears—while Carter offered a more rock-oriented approach on his *Now or Never*.

"Of course it's gonna change from what we were and what we've done," Carter said. "I don't mind having to go out there and prove myself and do something different."

And both singers predicted that their solo efforts would make an impact on their groups. Timberlake, for instance, cautioned that "The bubble-gum sound—I don't think people want to hear that anymore...The challenge is going to be trying to get a certain kind of focus on a certain kind of sound. I think we'll rise to the challenge."

Carter, meanwhile, says that the older members of Backstreet Boys need to be braced for a change as well. "We're gonna definitely have to change some things around when it comes to the music. Hopefully I can bring a new vibe to the band. It's almost like somebody stepping out of their family for a little bit and going to college or something, increasing their knowledge towards whatever they want."

Rocking On

Danny & the Juniors' late '50s sentiment that "Rock 'n' roll is here to stay/It will never die" rang true in 2002 thanks to a rash of fresh, guitar-toting talent that even included pop chart successes such as the aforementioned Avril Lavigne and Michelle Branch. But the year's "movement" was the so-called garage rock resurgence, in which seeming scores of bands beginning their names with The—The White Stripes, The Hives, The Vines, The Strokes—were embraced by the arbiters of hip and cool.

"I think garage rock means innocence," explained The White Stripes' Jack White. "That was a big part of what we're about, just playing the kind of music we want to and not really worrying about it in commercial or kind of industry terms."

White added that he didn't think all of these bands fit under one particular umbrella, but he acknowledged that "people just need a new tag for things, especially when they become popular. They need a name like grunge or new wave or punk rock. So let 'em call it garage rock; the name's been around for 40 years, anyway, so why not?"

Nicholaus Arson of The Hives said he felt many of these bands "do listen to a lot of the same music, but they all come up with different conclusions. It's not like they all sound the same. I think the 'scene' thing is kind of weird."

And The Strokes' Fabrizio Moretti said his band studiously avoids being pigeon-holed simply by not paying attention to what it felt were artificial groupings. "We just make our music according to how we think it sounds good," Moretti said, "and we don't really like to listen to the press influence or put ourselves in categories or anything like that."

Garage wasn't the only thing going on in rock during 2002, as exuberant youth and wily veterans all notched chart and radio successes. Canada's Nickelback continued to set the mark with hits such as "Never Again" and "Too Bad," while frontman Chad Kroeger teamed up with Saliva's Josey Scott for the smash "Hero" from the film soundtrack to *Spider-Man*. Contemporary punkers Good Charlotte sang about "Lifestyles of the Rich and Famous," while P.O.D. led the headbanging chant for the "Youth of the Nation." Slipknot, the costumed metal outfit from Iowa, took a hiatus that led to some side projects from its members—of which Stone Sour was the most successful with the unexpectedly mellow hit "Bother."

With Radiohead taking time off after the adventurous twin releases *Kid A* and *Amnesiac*, Coldplay rushed into the British band void with its sophomore album, *A Rush of Blood to the Head*, introducing it with the single "In My Place" and building its own momentum for a strong 2003.

"To be honest, the only pressure we felt was from ourselves, to try and do something melodic and passionate but also different and reflecting the new things we're into," Coldplay frontman Chris Martin said when talking about following up the group's five-million selling debut *Parachutes*. "While we're making [the album] we don't think of anybody but ourselves. We may live to regret that, but that's how we approach it, for better or for worse."

Rock's heavy side was bolstered in 2002 by the arrival of Audioslave, a super-group-style merger of three-quarters of Rage Against the Machine with former Soundgarden frontman Chris Cornell. The roiling "Cochise" got the group's self-titled debut album off to a strong start, and guitarist Tom Morello said that it was most important for fans to realize that "this is a band, not a *project*.

"When we first sat down with Chris," Morello explained, "it was really the conscious effort that we were not going to attempt to match people's expectations—we were going to defy people's expectations by starting from scratch. Our concern was 'What does a band sound like with we four as musicians?', not necessarily a band with this history as flagships of different genres of music, but what does it sound like when we get together and start writing songs as this singer, this guitar player, this bass player and this drummer. And it was pretty instantaneous and undeniable from the first day."

The old guys showed they could keep up, too. Tom Petty & the Heartbreakers and Elvis Costello released potent albums—*The Last DJ* and *When I Was Cruel*, respectively—while Peter Gabriel resurfaced after a 10-year recording break with *Up*. Santana's *Shaman* again paired him with younger collaborators such as Michelle Branch, Nickelback's Chad Kroeger and P.O.D.—plus opera tenor Placido Domingo—while the late George Harrison's posthumous effort, *Brainwashed*, was an understated delight. And former Led Zeppelin frontman Robert Plant—pocketing licensing fees from Cadillac for the use of his old band's "Rock and Roll" in ads—offered a group of inventive cover songs on his *Dreamland* album.

Plant was also pleased with a new version of Led Zep's "Stairway to Heaven"—this one recorded in bluegrass style by Dolly Parton. The music industry may have seemed all akimbo in some respects, but it was bold and divine moments like this that kept us listening.

—Gary Graff
Editor

A

Addicted to Bass
Words and music by Puretone (pseudonym for Josh Abrahams) and
Amiel Daemion
Universal Polygram International Pub., 2002
Performed by Puretone on the album *Stuck in a Groove* (V2, 2002).

Addictive
Words and music by David Blake, Stephen Garrett, Rakim (pseudonym
for William Griffin), and William Nichols
Bill-Lee Music, 2002/Cherry River Music, 2002/Frankly Music, 2002/
Music in Three, 2002/Herbilicious Music, 2002/Eighteenth Letter
Music, 2002/Songs of Dreamworks, 2002/Q Baby Music, 2002/
Lehsem Songs, 2002
Performed by Truth Hurts featuring Rakim on the album *Truthfully
Speaking* (Interscope, 2002).

Adrenaline
Words and music by Gavin Rossdale and Glen Ballard
JR Distribution Music, 2002/Aerostation Corp., 2002/Universal-MCA
Music Publishing, 2002
Performed by Gavin Rossdale on the soundtrack album *XXX* (Universal,
2002).

Adrienne
Words and music by Alex Band and Aaron Kamin
Alex Band Music, 2001/Amedeo Music, 2001/Careers-BMG Music
Publishing, 2001
Performed by the Calling on the album *Camino Palmero* (RCA, 2001).

Aeriels
Words and music by Serj Tankian, music by Daron Malakian and
Shavarsh Odadjian
Ddevil Music, 2001/Sony ATV Tunes LLC, 2001
Performed by System of a Down on the album *Toxicity* (American/

1

Columbia, 2001). Nominated for a Grammy Award, Best Hard Rock Performance, 2002.

Ain't It Funny
Words and music by Jennifer Lopez, Cadillac Tah (pseudonym for Cory Rooney), Ja Rule (pseudonym for Jeffrey Atkins), and Irv Gotti (pseudonym for Irving Lorenzo)
EMI-April Music, 2002/Obo Itself, 2002/Bee Mo Easy Music, 2002/ Justin Combs Publishing, 2002/Alvin Toney Music, 2002/Four Ya Ear Music, 2002/Nuyorican Publishing, 2002/Sony ATV Songs LLC, 2002/Cori Tiffani Publishing, 2002/DJ Irv Publishing, 2002/Ensign Music, 2002/Famous Music, 2002/Songs of Universal, 2002/White Rhino Music, 2002/Blunts Guns and Funds, 2002/Slavery Music, 2002
Performed by Jennifer Lopez featuring Ja Rule and Caddillac Tah on the album *J to tha L-O!: The Remixes* (Epic, 2002).

Ain't Nobody (We Got It Locked!)
Words by Ali Adams, Kelvyn Athouriste, Derek Johnson, Terrance Sanders, and Barrington Tulloch, music by Frederick Tulloch
Cross the Water Publishing, 2001
Performed by the Rawlo Boys featuring T.O.R.O. and Lil' Smoke. Released as a single.

Air Force Ones
Words and music by Nelly (pseudonym for Cornell Haynes), Murphy Lee (pseudonym for Tohri Harper), Ali Jones, and Robert Kyjuan Cleveland, music by Joe Kent and Mark Williams
Tarpo Music Publishing, London, England, 2002/BMG Songs, 2002/ Universal-MCA Music Publishing, 2002/Jackie Frost Music, 2002/Da Bess Music, 2002/Supreme Lee Music, 2002/Young Dude Music, 2002
Performed by Nelly featuring Kyjuan, Ali, and Murphy Lee on the album *Nellyville* (Universal, 2002).

Alive
Words and music by Tony Moran, Jeff Dorta, Kevin Aviance, Warren Rigg, and Ryan Shaw
Mr. Tan Man Music, 2002/BMG Music Publishing Ltd., 2002/Beyond the Beat Publishing, 2002/Largossa Music, 2002/B. Shaw Publishing, 2002
Performed by Kevin Aviance. Released as a single (Emerge, 2001).

Alive Again
Words and music by Ernest Anastasio, Scott Herman, and Thomas Marshall
Who Is She Music, 2002

Performed by Trey Anastasio on the album *Trey Anastasio* (Elektra, 2002).

All Eyez on Me
Words and music by Monica Arnold, LaShawn Daniels, James Ingram, Freddie Jerkins, Rodney Jerkins, and Quincy Jones
EMI-Blackwood Music, 2002/Ensign Music, 2002/Rodney Jerkins Productions, 2002/Warner-Tamerlane Publishing, 2002/Yellowbrick Road Music, 2002/Eiseman & Associates, 2002/Fred Jerkins Publishing, 2002
Performed by Monica on the album *All Eyez on Me* (J, 2002).

All My Life
Words and music by David Grohl, Oliver Taylor Hawkins, Nate Mendel, and Christopher Shiflett
Living Under a Rock Music, 2002/EMI-Virgin Songs, 2002/Flying Earform Music, 2002/I Love the Punk Rock Music, 2002/MJ Twelve Music, 2002
Performed by Foo Fighters on the album *One by One* (RCA, 2002). Won a Grammy Award for Best Hard Rock Performance, 2002. Nominated for a Grammy Award, Best Rock Song, 2002.

All the Pretty Girls Go to the City
Words and music by Britt Daniel
Henry Neuman Songs, 2002
Performed by Spoon on the album *Kill the Moonlight* (Merge, 2002).

All the Way
Words and music by Brian McKnight
Cancelled Lunch Music, 2002/Polygram International Publishing, 2002
Performed by Kenny G featuring Brian McKnight on the album *Paradise* (Arista, 2002). Nominated for a Grammy Award, Best R&B Performance by a Duo or Group With Vocal, 2002.

All You Wanted
Words and music by Michelle Branch
I'm With the Band Music, 2001/WB Music, 2001
Performed by Michelle Branch on the album *The Spirit Room* (Warner Bros., 2001).

Alone
Words and music by Tommy Sims
BMG Songs, 2000/Interscope Music Publishing, 2000/Bases Loaded Music, 2000
Covered by Susan Tedeschi on the album *Wait for Me* (Artemis, 2002). Originally performed by Tommy Sims on the album *Peace and Love* (Universal, 2000). Nominated for a Grammy Award, Best Female Rock Vocal Performance, 2002.

3

Always
Words and music by Paul Crosby, Christopher Dabaldo, Robert
    Marlette, David Novotny, Joseph Sappington, and Wayne Swinny
Almo Music, 2001/Black Lava, 2001/Five Superstars, 2001/Universal
    Music Publishing, 2001
Performed by Saliva on the album *Back Into Your System* (Def Jam,
    2002).

Always on Time
Words and music by Ja Rule (pseudonym for Jeffrey Atkins), Seven
    Aurelius, and Irv Gotti (pseudonym for Irving Lorenzo)
DJ Irv Publishing, 2001/Ensign Music, 2001/Slavery Music, 2001/Songs
    of Universal, 2001/White Rhino Music, 2001/Almo Music, 2001/
    Stygian Songs, 2001/Famous Music, 2001/Aurelius Publishing, 2001
Performed by Ja Rule featuring Ashanti on the album *Pain Is Love* (Def
    Jam, 2001). Nominated for a Grammy Award, Best Rap/Sung
    Collaboration, 2002.

Amber
Words and music by Nicholas Hexum
Hydroponic Music, 2001
Performed by 311 on the album *From Chaos* (Volcano, 2001).

America Will Always Stand
Words and music by Yvonne Blanton, Becki Blufield, Michael Curtis,
    Randy Travis (pseudonym for Randy Traywick), and Billy Walley
FMK, 2001/Major Bob Music, 2001/Sometimes You Win Music, 2001/
    Chrysalis Songs, 2001/Tennessee Hills Music, 2001
Performed by Randy Travis. Released as a single (Madacy, 2001).

American Child
Words and music by Phil Vassar and Craig Wiseman
BMG Songs, 2002/EMI-April Music, 2002/Mrs. Lumpkin's Poodle,
    2002
Performed by Phil Vassar on the album *American Child* (Arista, 2002).

American Girls
Words and music by Adam Duritz
EMI-Blackwood Music, 2002/Jones Falls Music, 2002
Performed by Counting Crows on the album *Hard Candy* (Geffen,
    2002).

Angels or Devils
Words by Gregg Wattenberg, words and music by John Richards, music
    by Scott Alexander, Rodney Cravens, Peter Maloney, and James
    Wood
600 Foot Hedgehog Music, 2002/EMI-April Music, 2002/Sniff It Music,
    2002/Sparkling Beatnik Music, 2002/Wu Shu Boy Music, 2002/Mono

Rat Music, 2002/T H I O, 2002
Performed by Dishwalla on the album *Opaline* (Immergent, 2002).

Anger Rising
Words and music by Jerry Cantrell
Boggy Bottom Publishing, 2002
Performed by Jerry Cantrell on the album *Degradation Trip*
(Roadrunner, 2002).

Any Day Now, also known as **My Wild Beautiful Bird**
Words and music by Bob Hilliard and Burt Bacharach
Bourne Co., 1962/New Hidden Valley Music, 1962
Covered by Luther Vandross on the album *Luther Vandross* (J, 2001).
Originally performed by Chuck Jackson. Nominated for a Grammy
Award, Best Traditional R&B Vocal Performance, 2002.

Anything
Words and music by Keir Gist, Robert Huggar, and Falonte Moore
Divine Mill Music, 2001/Lonte Music, 2001/WB Music, 2001/Uh Oh
Entertainment, 2001/Famous Music, 2001
Performed by Jaheim featuring Next on the album *Ghetto Love* (Warner
Bros., 2001).

Apollo
Music by Tony Levin
T-Lev Music, 2002
Performed by Tony Levin on the album *Pieces of the Sun* (Narada,
2002). Nominated for a Grammy Award, Best Rock Instrumental
Performance, 2002.

Approaching Pavonis Mons by Balloon (Utopia Planitia)
Music by Michael Ivins, Wayne Coyne, and Steven Drozd
EMI-Blackwood Music, 2002/Lovely Sorts of Death Music, 2002
Performed by the Flaming Lips on the album *Yoshimi Battles the Pink
Robots* (Warner Bros., 2002). Won a Grammy Award for Best Rock
Instrumental Performance, 2002.

Are We Cuttin'
Words and music by Timbaland (pseudonym for Timothy Mosley),
Pastor Troy (pseudonym for Micah Troy), and Ms. Jade (pseudonym
for Chevon Young)
Virginia Beach Music, 2002/WB Music, 2002/Pastor Troy, 2002
Performed by Pastor Troy featuring Ms. Jade (Universal, 2002). Initially
released as a single; later featured on the album *Universal Soldier*
(Universal, 2002).

Are You Passionate?
Words and music by Neil Young
Silver Fiddle Music, 2002

Performed by Neil Young on the album *Are You Passionate?* (Reprise, 2002).

As It Is
Music by Lyle Mays and Pat Metheny
Lyle Mays Music, 2002/Pat Meth Music, 2002
Performed by the Pat Metheny Group on the album *Speaking of Now* (Warner Bros., 2002). Nominated for a Grammy Award, Best Pop Instrumental Performance, 2002.

Asereje, see **The Ketchup Song (Hey Hah)**.

Auld Lang Syne
Traditional
Performed by B.B. King on the album *A Christmas Celebration of Hope* (MCA, 2001). Instrumental version of traditional New Year's song. Won a Grammy Award for Best Pop Instrumental Performance, 2002.

Awnaw
Words and music by Vito Tisdale, Melvin Adams, Kenneth Anthony, W. Chambers, and William Hughes
Universal Music Publishing, 2002/Nappy Roots Publishing, 2002
Performed by Nappy Roots featuring Jazze Pha on the album *Watermelon, Chicken and Gritz* (Atlantic, 2002).

B

Baby
Words and music by Michael Dean, Ashanti Douglas, Brad Jordan, Irv
  Gotti (pseudonym for Irving Lorenzo), and Andre Parker
Famous Music, 2002/N The Water Publishing, 2002/Pookietoots
  Publishing, 2002/Universal Polygram International Pub., 2002/DJ Irv
  Publishing, 2002/Ensign Music, 2002
Performed by Ashanti on the album *Ashanti* (Murder Inc., 2002).

Ballin' Boy
Words and music by Derrick Hill and Tracy Latimer
No Good But So Good Music, 2002
Performed by No Good on the album *Game Day, PBB* (Artist Direct,
  2002).

Barenaked
Words and music by Meredith Brooks, Guy Erez, Jennifer Love-Hewitt,
  Emerson Swinford, and Paul Goldowitz
In Love, 2002/Sababa G, 2002/Swinstone, 2002/Zomba Enterprises,
  2002/EMI-Blackwood Music, 2002/Kissing Booth Music, 2002
Performed by Jennifer Love-Hewitt on the album *BareNaked* (Jive,
  2002).

The Barry Williams Show
Words and music by Peter Gabriel
Pentagon Lipservices Real World, 2002/Real World Music (PRS), 2002
Performed by Peter Gabriel on the album *Up* (Geffen, 2002). Nominated
  for a Grammy Award, Best Male Rock Vocal Performance, 2002.

Basketball
Words and music by James Bralower, Robert Ford, James Moore, Kurtis
  Blow (pseudonym for Kurt Walker), Shirley Walker, and William
  Waring
Fancy Footwork Music, 1984/Mofunk Music, 1984/Neutral Gray Music,
  1984/Original JB Music, 1984
Covered by Lil' Bow Wow featuring Fabolous and Jermaine Dupri on

the soundtrack album *Like Mike* (So So Def, 2002). Originally performed by Kurtis Blow on the album *Ego Trip* (Mercury, 1984).

Be Here, also known as **You Should Be Here**
Words and music by D'Angelo (pseudonym for Michael D'Angelo Archer), Robert Ozuna, Raphael Saadiq, and Glenn Standridge
Ah Choo Music, 2002/Jake and the Phatman Music, 2002/Ugmoe Music, 2002/Universal Polygram International Pub., 2002
Performed by Raphael Saadiq featuring D'Angelo on the album *Instant Vintage* (Universal, 2002). Nominated for Grammy Awards, Best R&B Song, 2002, and Best Urban/Alternative Performance, 2002.

Bear Mountain Hop
Music by Bela Fleck
Walt Disney Music Co., 2002/Fleck Music, 2002/Wonderland Music, 2002
Performed by Bela Fleck on the soundtrack album *The Country Bears* (Disney, 2002). Nominated for a Grammy Award, Best Country Instrumental Performance, 2002.

Bearing Straight
Music by Ilya Toshinsky, Lydia Salnikova, Sasha Ostrovsky, and Sergei Passov
Uncle Hadley Music, 2001
Performed by Bering Strait on the album *Bering Strait* (Universal South, 2003). Nominated for a Grammy Award, Best Country Instrumental Performance, 2002.

Beautiful Mess
Words and music by Alfred Lemaire, Clay Mills, and Shane Minor
Chrysalis Music, 2002/Creative Artists Agency, 2002/EMI-Blackwood Music, 2002/Monkey C Music, 2002/Shane Minor Music, 2002/Songs of API, 2002/Songs of Nashville Dreamworks, 2002
Performed by Diamond Rio on the album *Completely* (Arista, 2002). Nominated for a Grammy Award, Best Country Performance by a Duo/Group With Vocal, 2002.

Better Than Anything
Words by Bill Loughborough, music by David Wheat
Sanga Music, 1962
Covered by Natalie Cole featuring Diana Krall on the album *Ask a Woman Who Knows* (Verve, 2002). Originally performed by Irene Kral on the album *better than anything* (Ava, 1963). Nominated for a Grammy Award, Best Pop Collaboration With Vocals, 2002.

Black Suits Comin' (Nod Ya Head)
Words and music by Lance Bennett, Lemar Bennett, Lennie Bennett, Ronald Feemster, Willard Smith, and Mark Sparks

It Hurtz Music, 2002/Treyball Music, 2002/Da Fabulous BeatBrokers
  Music, 2002/Love N Loyalty Music, 2002/Blitz Package Music, 2002
Performed by Will Smith featuring TRA-Knox on the soundtrack album
  Men in Black (Columbia, 2002). Also included on Smith's album
  Born to Reign (Columbia, 2002).

Blackbird
Words and music by John Lennon and Paul McCartney
Sony ATV Tunes LLC, 1968
Covered by Dave Koz and Jeff Koz on the album *Golden Slumbers: A
  Father's Lullaby* (Warner Bros., 2002). Originally performed by the
  Beatles on the album *The Beatles* (Capitol, 1968). Nominated for a
  Grammy Award, Best Pop Instrumental Performance, 2002.

Blessed
Words and music by Brett James, Hillary Lindsey, and Troy Verges
Songs of Universal, 2001/Animal Fair, 2001/Famous Music, 2001/Sony
  ATV Tunes LLC, 2001/Teracel Music, 2001
Performed by Martina McBride on the album *Greatest Hits* (RCA,
  2001). Nominated for a Grammy Award, Best Female Country Vocal
  Performance, 2002.

Blurry
Words and music by Wesley Scantlin, James Allen, and Douglas Ardito
Jordan Rocks Music, 2001/Stereo Supersonic Music, 2001/WB Music,
  2001/The Thick Plottens Music, 2001
Performed by Puddle of Mudd on the album *Come Clean* (Flawless,
  2001).

Bother
Words and music by Corey Taylor
EMI-April Music, 2002/Music That Music, 2002
Performed by Stone Sour on the album *Stone Sour* (Roadrunner, 2002).

Bouncin' Back (Bumpin' Me Against the Wall)
Words and music by Charles Hugo, Mystikal (pseudonym for Michael
  Tyler), and Pharrell Williams
Chase Chad Music, 2001/EMI-April Music, 2001/The Braids Publishing,
  2001/EMI-Blackwood Music, 2001/Waters of Nazareth Publishing,
  2001
Performed by Mystikal on the album *Tarantula* (Jive, 2001). Nominated
  for a Grammy Award, Best Male Rap Solo Performance, 2002.

Boys
Words and music by Charles Hugo and Pharrell Williams
EMI-Blackwood Music, 2001/Waters of Nazareth Publishing, 2001/
  Chase Chad Music, 2001
Performed by Britney Spears on the album *Britney* (Jive, 2001)

Braid My Hair
Words and music by Warryn Campbell and Harold Lilly
EMI-Blackwood Music, 2002/Uncle Bobby Music, 2002
Performed by Mario on the album *Mario* (J, 2002).

Break You Off
Words and music by James Gray, Hub (pseudonym for Leonard
    Hubbard), Musiq (pseudonym for Talib Johnson), Kyle Jones,
    Benjamin Kenney, Jill Scott, ?uestlove (pseudonym for Amir
    Thompson), and Black Thought (pseudonym for Tarik Trotter)
Killah Stealth Music, 2002/One CRC Publishing, 2002
Performed by the Roots featuring Musiq on the album *Phrenology*
    (MCA, 2002).

Breathe Your Name
Words and music by Matthew Slocum
My So Called Music, 2002/Squint Songs, 2002
Performed by Sixpence None the Richer on the album *Divine Discontent*
    (Squint/Reprise, 2002).

Bridge Over Troubled Water
Words and music by Paul Simon
Paul Simon Music, 1969
Covered by Johnny Cash featuring Fiona Apple on the album *American
    IV: The Man Comes Around* (Universal, 2002). Originally performed
    by Simon and Garfunkel on the album *Bridge Over Troubled Water*
    (Columbia, 1970.) Nominated for a Grammy Award, Best Country
    Collaboration With Vocals, 2002.

Bring on the Rain
Words and music by Billy Montana and Helen Darling
Bro N' Sis Music, 2000/Estes Park Music, 2000/Little Chatterbox
    Music, 2000/Mike Curb Music, 2000/Warner-Tamerlane Publishing,
    2000
Performed by Jo Dee Messina featuring Tim McGraw on the album
    Burn (Curb, 2000).

Burn It Blue
Words by Julie Taymor, music by Elliot Goldenthal
Zarathustra Music, 2002/MRX Music, 2002
Performed by Caetano Veloso and Lila Downs on the soundtrack album
    Frida (Universal, 2002). Nominated for an Academy Award, Best
    Original Song, 2002.

By the Way
Words and music by Flea (pseudonym for Michael Balzary), John
    Frusciante, Anthony Kiedis, and Chad Smith
Moebetoblame Music, 2002

Performed by Red Hot Chili Peppers on the album *By the Way* (Warner Bros., 2002).

Bye-Bye Baby
Words and music by Brandy Scott
Jesus Never Fails Publishing, 2002
Performed by Brandy Moss-Scott on the album *Fresh* (Heavenly Tunes, 2002).

C

Call Me
Words and music by Tweet (pseudonym for Charlene Keys) and
  Timbaland (pseudonym for Timothy Mosley)
Fo Shawna Productions, 2002/Virginia Beach Music, 2002/WB Music,
  2002
Performed by Tweet on the album *Southern Hummingbird* (Goldmind/
  Elektra, 2002).

Can I Get That?!!?
Words and music by Jeremy Watkins, words by Jorick Newberry and
  Joseph Newberry
Headquarters Records, 2001
Performed by Bear Witnez! Released as a single.

Can't Fight the Moonlight
Words and music by Diane Warren
Realsongs, 2000
Performed by LeAnn Rimes on the soundtrack album *Coyote Ugly*
  (Curb, 2002). Also included on Rimes' album *I Need You* (Curb,
  2001).

Can't Get You out of My Head
Words and music by Rob Davis and Cathy Dennis
EMI Music Publishing Ltd., 2002/Universal Music Publishing Int. Ltd.,
  2002
Performed by Kylie Minogue on the album *Fever* (Capitol, 2002).

Can't Stop Dancin'
Words and music by Brian Banuolo, Michael Cruz, and Inaya Day
  (pseudonym for Jafan Davis)
Jessica Michael Music, 2001/NY O'Dae Music, 2001
Performed by Inaya Day on the album *The Cuts: Session 001* (Strictly
  Rhythm, 2001).

Caramel
Words by Charles Young, words and music by Robert Pardlo, Ryan Toby, Ahmir Thompson, Scott Storch, Hub (pseudonym for Leonard Hubbard), and Tarik Collins, music by Jerry Duplessis and Giscard Xavier
EMI-April Music, 2001/Noclist Music, 2001/Pladis Music, 2001/ Careers-BMG Music Publishing, 2001/EMI-Blackwood Music, 2001/Te Bass Music, 2001
Performed by City High featuring Eve on the album *City High* (Interscope, 2001).

Castles in the Sky
Words and music by Christophe Chantzis, Martine Theeuwen, and Marc Vanspauwen
Rocks LLC, 2002
Performed by Ian Van Dahl featuring Marsha on the album *Ace* (Robbins, 2002).

Ching Ching
Words and music by Gerald Eaton, Nelly Furtado, Garland Mosley, Timbaland (pseudonym for Timothy Mosley), Brian West, and Ms. Jade (pseudonym for Chevon Young)
757 Music, 2002/Virginia Beach Music, 2002/WB Music, 2002/Sony ATV Songs LLC, 2002/Mawga Dawg, 2002/Worldwide West Music, 2002/Nelstar Publishing, 2002
Performed by Ms. Jade featuring Nelly Furtado and Timbaland on the album *Girl Interrupted* (Interscope, 2002).

Christmas Song
Words and music by Melvin Torme and Robert Wells
Edwin H. Morris, 1946
Performed by India.Arie and Stevie Wonder on a special edition of the album *Voyage to India* (Motown, 2002) only available through Target stores. Nominated for a Grammy Award, Best Pop Collaboration With Vocals, 2002.

Cleanin out My Closet
Words and music by Eminem (pseudonym for Marshall Mathers) and Jeffrey Bass
Eight Mile Style Music, 2002/Ensign Music, 2002
Performed by Eminem on the album *The Eminem Show* (Aftermath/ Interscope, 2002).

Cochise
Words and music by Christopher Cornell, music by Timothy Commerford, Thomas Morello, and Brad Wilks
Disappearing One, 2002/LBV Songs, 2002/Me Three Publishing, 2002/

Melee Savvy Music, 2002/Wixen Music Publishing, 2002
Performed by Audioslave on the album *Audioslave* (Epic, 2002).

The Color of Love
Words and music by Babyface (pseudonym for Kenneth Edmonds)
Ecaf Music, 2002/Sony ATV Songs LLC, 2002
Performed by Boyz II Men on the album *Full Circle* (Arista, 2002).

Combat Rock
Words and music by Carrie Brownstein, Corin Tucker, and Janet Weiss
Code Word Nemesis, Olympia, 2002
Performed by Sleater-Kinney on the album *One Beat* (Kill Rock Stars, 2002.)

Come Close, also known as **Come Close to Me**
Words by Common (pseudonym for Lonnie Lynn), music by Charles
    Hugo and Pharrell Williams
EMI-Blackwood Music, 2002/Senseless Music, 2002/Songs of
    Universal, 2002/Waters of Nazareth Publishing, 2002
Performed by Common featuring Mary J. Blige on the album *Electric
    Circus* (MCA, 2002).

Come Close to Me, see **Come Close**.

Como Duele
Words and music by Armando Manzanero
D Nico International, 2001
Performed by Luis Miguel on the album *Mis Romance* (WEA
    International, 2001).

Complicated
Words and music by Scott Spock (pseudonym for David Alspach),
    Graham Edwards, Lauren Christy (pseudonym for Lauren Fownes),
    and Avril Lavigne
Almo Music, 2002/Ferry Hill Songs, 2002/WB Music, 2002/Mr. Spock
    Music, 2002/Rainbow Fish Publishing, 2002/Warner-Tamerlane
    Publishing, 2002
Performed by Avril Lavigne on the album *Let Go* (Arista, 2002).
    Nominated for Grammy Awards, Best Female Pop Vocal
    Performance, 2002, and Song of the Year, 2002.

Count It Off
Words and music by J. Brown, Jay-Z (pseudonym for Shawn Carter),
    Timbaland (pseudonym for Timothy Mosley), and Ms. Jade
    (pseudonym for Chevon Young)
Crited Music, 2002/Dynatone Publishing, 2002/Virginia Beach Music,
    2002/Lil Lu Lu Publishing, 2002
Performed by Ms. Jade featuring Jay-Z on the album *Girl Interrupted*
    (Interscope, 2002).

Courtesy of the Red, White and Blue (The Angry American)
Words and music by Toby Keith (pseudonym for Toby Covel)
Tokeco Tunes, 2002
Performed by Toby Keith on the album *Unleashed* (DreamWorks,
    2002).

Cowboy
Words and music by Eve (pseudonym for Eve Jeffers) and Fatboy Slim
    (pseudonym for Quentin Cook)
Blondie Rockwell Music, 2000/Universal Music Publishing, 2000/
    Universal Polygram International Pub., 2000
Performed by Eve featuring Fatboy Slim on the soundtrack album *Blade
    II* (Virgin, 2002). Originally appeared on Eve's album *Scorpion*
    (Interscope, 2000).

The Cowboy in Me
Words and music by Alan Anderson, Jeffrey Steele, and Craig Wiseman
BMG Songs, 2001/Mrs. Lumpkin's Poodle, 2001/Gottahaveable Music,
    2001/Songs of Windswept Pacific, 2001/Stairway to Bittner's Music,
    2001
Performed by Tim McGraw on the album *Set This Circus Down* (Curb,
    2001).

Crawling in the Dark
Words and music by Daniel Estrin, Chris Hesse, Markku Lappalainen,
    and Douglas Robb
Spread Your Cheeks, 2001/WB Music, 2001
Performed by Hoobastank on the soundtrack album *More Music from
    The Fast and the Furious* (Island/Def Jam, 2001). Also included on
    Hoobastank's album *Hoobastank* (Universal, 2001).

Crush Tonight
Words and music by Fat Joe (pseudonym for Joseph Cartagena), John
    Eaddy, Larry Gate, Elgin Lumpkin, A. Lyon, and Marcello Valenzano
Jelly's Jams LLC Music, 2002/Music of Windswept, 2002/Hand in My
    Pocket Music, 2002/Shelly's House Music, 2002/Joseph Cartagena
    Music, 2002/EMI-April Music, 2002
Performed by Fat Joe featuring Ginuwine on the album *Loyalty*
    (Atlantic, 2002).

Cry
Words and music by Angie Aparo
Potty Mouth Publishing, 2000/Warner-Tamerlane Publishing, 2000/
    Round Tower Publishing, 2000
Covered by Faith Hill on the album *Cry* (Warner Bros., 2002).
    Originally performed by Angie Aparo on the album *The American*
    (Arista, 2000). Won a Grammy Award for Best Female Country
    Vocal Performance, 2002.

Cry on Demand
Words and music by Ryan Adams
Barland Music, 2001
Performed by Ryan Adams on the album *Demolition* (Lost Highway, 2002).

D

Dagger Through the Heart
Words and music by Dolly Parton
Velvet Apple Music, 2002
Performed by Dolly Parton on the album *Halos & Horns* (Sugar Hill, 2002). Nominated for a Grammy Award, Best Female Country Vocal Performance, 2002.

Darkness
Words and music by Dan Donegan, David Draiman, Fuzz (pseudonym for Steve Kmak), and Michael Wengren
Mother Culture Publishing, 2002/WB Music, 2002
Performed by Disturbed on the album *Believe* (Warner Bros., 2002).

Darkness, Darkness
Words and music by Jesse Colin Young (pseudonym for Perry Miller)
Pigfoot Music, 1969
Covered by Robert Plant on the album *Dreamland* (Universal, 2002). Song originally performed by the Youngbloods on the album *Elephant Mountain* (RCA, 1969). Nominated for a Grammy Award, Best Male Rock Vocal Performance, 2002.

Days Go By
Words and music by Victoria Horn and Steven Smith
EMI-Blackwood Music, 2001/Chrysalis Music, 2001
Performed by Dirty Vegas on the album *Dirty Vegas* (Capitol, 2002). Originally appeared on the compilation album *I Love Ibiza* (EMI, 2001). Won a Grammy Award for Best Dance Recording, 2002. Nominated for a Grammy Award, Best Short Form Music Video, 2002.

Dear God
Words by Willie Dennis, music by Leroy Edwards
Geto Boys and Girls Music, 2000/Mighty Nice Music, 2000/Still N The Water Publishing, 2000
Performed by Willie D on the album on the album *Relentless*

(Relentless, 2001). Originally appeared on D's album *Loved by Few, Hated by Many* (Virgin, 2000).

Diary
Words and music by Charli Baltimore (pseudonym for Tiffany Lane), Irv Gotti (pseudonym for Irving Lorenzo), and Andre Parker
DJ Irv Publishing, 2002/Ensign Music, 2002/Inky Sisi Music, 2002/Un Rivera Publishing, 2002/Warner-Tamerlane Publishing, 2002
Performed by Charli Baltimore on the album *The Diary* (Universal, 2002). Nominated for a Grammy Award, Best Female Rap Solo Performance, 2002.

Die Another Day
Words and music by Madonna Ciccone and Mirwais Ahmadzai
Webo Girl Publishing, 2002/1000 Lights Music Ltd., 2002
Performed by Madonna on the soundtrack album *Die Another Day* (Warner Bros., 2002).

A Different Kind of Love Song
Words and music by Johan Aberg, Michelle Lewis, and Sigurd Roesnes
BMG Songs, 2002/Wannabite Music, 2002
Performed by Cher on the album *Living Proof* (Warner Bros., 2002).

Dilemma
Words by Nelly (pseudonym for Cornell Haynes), Kenneth Gamble, and Walter Sigler, music by Antoine Macon
Warner-Tamerlane Publishing, 2002/BMG Songs, 2002/EMI-April Music, 2002/Shack Suga Entertainment, 2002/Jackie Frost Music, 2002/Phat Nasty Publishing, 2002
Performed by Nelly featuring Kelly Rowland on the album *Nellyville* (Universal, 2002). Won a Grammy Award for Best Rap/Sung Collaboration, 2002. Nominated for a Grammy Award, Record of the Year, 2002.

Dirrty
Words and music by Christina Aguilera, Jasper Cameron, Bale'wa Muhammad, Reggie Noble, and Dana Stinson
Funky Noble Productions, 2002/WB Music, 2002/Careers-BMG Music Publishing, 2002/Dayna's Day Publishing, 2002/Ostaf Songs, 2002/Warner-Tamerlane Publishing, 2002/Xtina Music, 2002
Performed by Christina Aguilera featuring Redman on the album *Stripped* (RCA, 2002). Nominated for a Grammy Award, Best Pop Collaboration With Vocals, 2002.

Disease
Words and music by Robert Thomas and Michael Jagger
Bidnis, 2002/EMI-Blackwood Music, 2002/Jagged Music, 2002

Performed by matchbox twenty on the album *More Than You Think You Are* (Atlantic, 2002).

Do It for Love
Words and music by Daryl Hall, John Oates, William Mann, and Paul Pesco
Careers-BMG Music Publishing, 2002/Hot Cha Music, 2002/Turtle Wins the Race, 2002/Annotation Music, 2002/Da Doo Da Publishing, 2002
Performed by Daryl Hall and John Oates on the album *Behind the Music: the Daryl Hall and John Oates Collection* (RCA, 2002).

Do You Realize?
Words and music by Michael Ivins, Wayne Coyne, Steven Drozd, and David Fridmann
EMI-Blackwood Music, 2002/Lovely Sorts of Death Music, 2002
Performed by the Flaming Lips on the album *Yoshimi Battles the Pink Robots* (Warner Bros., 2002).

Don't Know Why
Words and music by Jesse Harris
Beanly Songs, 2001/Sony ATV Songs LLC, 2001
Performed by Norah Jones on the album *Come Away With Me* (Blue Note, 2002). Song originally appeared on the EP *First Sessions* (Blue Note, 2001). Won Grammy Awards.

Don't Let Me Get Me, also known as **Hazard to Myself**
Words and music by Dallas Austin and Pink (pseudonym for Alecia Moore)
Cryptron Music, 2001/EMI-Blackwood Music, 2001/EMI-April Music, 2001/Pink Panther Music, 2001
Performed by Pink on the album *M!ssundaztood* (Arista, 2001).

Don't Mess With My Man
Words and music by Brandon Casey, Brian Casey, and Bryan Cox
Air Control Music, 2001/EMI-April Music, 2001/Them Damn Twins Music, 2001/Babyboys Little Pub Co, 2001
Performed by Nivea featuring Brian Casey and Brandon Casey on the album *Nivea* (Jive, 2001). Nominated for a Grammy Award, Best R&B Performance by a Duo or Group With Vocal, 2002.

Don't Stop
Words and music by Michael Jagger and Keith Richards
ABKCO Music, 2002
Performed by the Rolling Stones on the album *Forty Licks* (Virgin, 2002).

Don't You Forget It
Words and music by Glenn Lewis and Andre Harris
Dirty Dre Music, 2002/Jat Cat Music Publishing, 2002/Universal Music

Publishing, 2002/WB Music, 2002
Performed by Glenn Lewis on the album *World Outside My Window* (Epic, 2002).

Dontchange
Words and music by Ivan Barias, Carvin Haggins, Musiq (pseudonym for Talib Johnson), and Frank Romano
Jat Cat Music Publishing, 2002/Jessy Jaye Music, 2002/Soul Child Music, 2002/Tetragrammaton Music, 2002/Universal Music Publishing, 2002
Performed by Musiq on the album *Juslisen* (Def Soul, 2002).

Dope Nose
Words and music by Rivers Cuomo
E. O. Smith Music, 2002
Performed by Weezer on the album *Maladroit* (Interscope, 2002).

Down A** B**ch
Words and music by Ja Rule (pseudonym for Jeffrey Atkins), Seven Aurelius, Charli Baltimore (pseudonym for Tiffany Lane), and Irv Gotti (pseudonym for Irving Lorenzo)
DJ Irv Publishing, 2001/Ensign Music, 2001/Inky Sisi Music, 2001/ Slavery Music, 2001/Songs of Universal, 2001/Un Rivera Publishing, 2001/Warner-Tamerlane Publishing, 2001/White Rhino Music, 2001/ Almo Music, 2001/Stygian Songs, 2001
Performed by Ja Rule featuring Charli Baltimore on the album *Pain Is Love* (Def Jam, 2001).

Down 4 U
Words and music by Ja Rule (pseudonym for Jeffrey Atkins), Seven Aurelius, Ashanti Douglas, Tiffany Jarmon, Irv Gotti (pseudonym for Irving Lorenzo), Andre Parker, Larry Troutman, and Roger Troutman
DJ Irv Publishing, 2002/Ensign Music, 2002/Inky Sisi Music, 2002/Saja Music Co., 2002/Slavery Music, 2002/Songs of Lastrada, 2002/Sony ATV Songs LLC, 2002/Universal Songs of Polygram Intntl., 2002/ Warner-Tamerlane Publishing, 2002/Famous Music, 2002/Aurelius Publishing, 2002/Soldierz Touch, 2002/Pookietoots Publishing, 2002
Performed by Irv Gotti on the album *Irv Gotti Presents: The Inc.* (Def Jam, 2002).

Down the Road
Words and music by Van Morrison
Exile Publishing Ltd., 2002/Universal Music Publishing Int. Ltd., 2002
Performed by Van Morrison on the album *Down the Road* (Universal, 2002).

Downfall
Words and music by James Fukai, Joshua Moates, Kevin Palmer, and

Jason Singleton
Barely Breathing, 2002/Bright Gray Publishing, 2002/EMI-April Music, 2002
Performed by TRUST company on the album *The Lonely Position of Neutral* (Geffen, 2002).

Drift & Die
Words and music by Wesley Scantlin and James Allen
Jordan Rocks Music, 2001/Stereo Supersonic Music, 2001/WB Music, 2001
Performed by Puddle of Mudd on the album *Come Clean* (Flawless, 2001).

Drive (For Daddy Gene)
Words and music by Alan Jackson
EMI-April Music, 2002/Tri Angels Music, 2002
Performed by Alan Jackson on the album *Drive* (Arista, 2002).

E

18
Music by Moby (pseudonym for Richard Hall)
Little Idiot Music, 2002/Warner-Tamerlane Publishing, 2002
Performed by Moby on the album *18* (V2, 2002). Nominated for a
   Grammy Award, Best Pop Instrumental Performance, 2002.

Electrical Storm
Words and music by Bono (pseudonym for Paul Hewson), The Edge
   (pseudonym for David Evans), Adam Clayton, and Larry Mullen, Jr
Universal Polygram International Pub., 2002
Performed by U2 on the album *The Best of 1990-2000* (Interscope,
   2002).

The Empty Page
Words and music by Kim Gordon, Thurston Moore, Lee Ranaldo, and
   Steven Shelley
Field Code Music, 2001/Sonik Tooth Music, 2001
Performed by Sonic Youth on the album *Murray Street* (Interscope,
   2002).

Eple
Music by Sven Berge and Torbjorn Brundtland
Copyright Control Music, 2001
Performed by Royksopp on the album *Melody A.M.* (Astralwerks, 2001).

Escapar, see **Escape**.

Escape, also known as **Escapar**
Words and music by Kara Dioguardi, Enrique Iglesias, Steve Morales,
   and David Siegel
EMI-April Music, 2001/Enrique Iglesias Music, 2001/Jumping Bean
   Songs, 2001/K Stuff Publishing, 2001/Merchandyze Music, 2001/
   Million Dollar Steve Music, 2001/Warner-Tamerlane Publishing, 2001
Performed by Enrique Iglesias on the album *Escape* (Interscope, 2001).

The Essence
Words and music by AZ (pseudonym for Anthony Cruz), P. Hendricks, Rick James, J. Johnson, N. Jones, and M. Risko
Stone City Music, 2002/Baby Paul Muzik, 2002/Mike Wrecka Music, 2002
Performed by AZ featuring Nas on the album *Aziatic* (Motown, 2002). Nominated for a Grammy Award, Best Rap Performance by a Duo or Group, 2002.

Every River, also known as Every River Run Dry
Words and music by Kim Richey, Tom Littlefield, and Angelo (pseudonym for Angelo Petraglia)
Door Number One Music, 1997/Mighty Nice Music, 1997/Universal Songs of Polygram Intntl., 1997/Wait No More Music, 1997
Covered by Brooks & Dunn on the album *Steers & Stripes* (Arista, 2001). Originally performed by Kim Richey on the album *Bittersweet* (Polygram, 1997).

Every River Run Dry, see Every River.

Everyday
Words and music by John Bongiovi, Andreas Carlsson, and Richard Sambora
Aggressive Music, 2002/Bon Jovi Publishing, 2002/Universal Polygram International Pub., 2002/WB Music, 2002
Performed by Bon Jovi on the album *Bounce* (Island/Def Jam, 2002). Nominated for a Grammy Award, Best Pop Performance by a Duo or Group With Vocal, 2002.

Everything
Words and music by James Bralower, Marit Larsen, Marion Ravn, and Peter Zizzo
Fancy Footwork Music, 2002/WB Music, 2002/Connotation Music, 2002/Pez Music, 2002/Warner-Tamerlane Publishing, 2002
Performed by M2M on the album *The Big Room* (Atlantic, 2002).

F

Fabulous
Words and music by Edward Berkeley, Mary Brown, Victor
Carstarphen, Keir Gist, Jaheim Hoagland, Gene MacFadden, Bale'wa
Muhammad, and John Whitehead
Divine Mill Music, 2002/Fingas Goal Music, 2002/WB Music, 2002/Ms.
Mary's Music, 2002/Warner-Tamerlane Publishing, 2002
Performed by Jaheim featuring the Rayne on the album *Still Ghetto*
(Warner Bros., 2002).

Fall Into Me
Words and music by Dan Orton and Jeremy Stover
Halhana Music Publishing, 2002/Platinum Plow, 2002/Universal-MCA
Music Publishing, 2002/WB Music, 2002
Performed by Emerson Drive on the album *Emerson Drive*
(DreamWorks, 2002).

Fame 02
Words and music by Carlos Alomar, David Bowie (pseudonym for
David Jones), and John Lennon
Chrysalis Music, 1975/Colgems EMI Music, 1975/Jones Music America,
1975/Unitunes Music, 1975/Lenono Music, 1975
Covered by Tommy Lee on the soundtrack album *The Banger Sisters*
(Sanctuary, 2002). Also included on Lee's album *Never a Dull
Moment* (MCA, 2002). Originally performed by David Bowie on the
album *Young Americans* (RCA, 1975).

Father and Daughter
Words and music by Paul Simon
Paul Simon Music, 2002
Performed by Paul Simon on the soundtrack album *The Wild
Thornberrys Movie* (Jive, 2002). Nominated for an Academy Award,
Best Original Song, 2002.

Feel It Girl
Words and music by Pharrell Williams, Moses Davis, and Charles Hugo

Chase Chad Music, 2002/EMI-April Music, 2002/EMI-Blackwood
Music, 2002/Waters of Nazareth Publishing, 2002
Performed by Beenie Man featuring Janet Jackson on the album
Tropical Storm (Virgin, 2002).

Feels Good (Don't Worry Bout a Thing)
Words and music by Vincent Brown, Anthony Criss, Clemon Riley,
Raphael Saadiq, Carl Wheeler, Teron Beal, Allen Gordon, Dwayne
Wiggins, and Nastacia Kendall
Tony Toni Tone Music, 1990/Universal Polygram International Pub.,
1990/Mytrell Publishing, 1990
Covered by Naughty by Nature featuring 3LW on the album *Iicons*
(TVT, 2002). Originally performed by Tony Toni Tone on the album
Revival (Wing, 1990).

Fight Song
Words and music by George Livengood and Gretchen Lykins
Crack Rock Music, 2002
Performed by Jucifer on the album *I Name You Destroyer* (Velocette,
2002).

Fine Again
Words and music by Shaun Morgan, music by Dale Stewart
Seether Publishing, 2002/Dwight Frye Music, 2002
Performed by Seether on the album *Disclaimer* (Wind-Up, 2002).

First Date
Words and music by Travis Barker, Thomas Delonge, and Mark Hoppus
EMI-April Music, 2001/Fun With Goats Music, 2001
Performed by blink-182 on the album *Take Off Your Pants and Jacket*
(MCA, 2001).

Fishin' Song, see I'm Gonna Miss Her.

Flesh and Blood
Words and music by John Cash
Song of Cash, 1969
Covered by Mary Chapin Carpenter, Sheryl Crow and Emmylou Harris
on the album *Kindred Spirits: A Tribute to the Songs of Johnny Cash*
(Sony, 2002). Originally performed by Johnny Cash. Nominated for a
Grammy Award, Best Country Collaboration With Vocals, 2002.

Float Away
Words and music by Dave Bielanko, Derge Bielanko, Kenneth Gamble,
and Leon Huff
Rykomusic, 2002
Performed by Marah on the album *Float Away With the Friday Night
Gods* (Artemis, 2002).

Floetic
Words by Marsha Ambrosius and Natalie Stewart, words and music by
   Melvin Torme and Robert Wells, music by Darren Henson and Keith
   Pelzer
SPZ Music, London, England, 2002/EMI-April Music, 2002/Jat Cat
   Music Publishing, 2002/Jay Qui Music, 2002/Jewel Music Publishing,
   2002/No Gravity Music, 2002/Touched by Jazz Music, 2002/Wells
   Music, 2002
Performed by Floetry on the album *Floetic* (DreamWorks, 2002).
   Nominated for Grammy Awards, Best R&B Song, 2002, and Best
   Urban/Alternative Performance, 2002.

Foolish
Words and music by Seven Aurelius, Ashanti Douglas, and Irv Gotti
   (pseudonym for Irving Lorenzo), music by Mark DeBarge and Bunny
   DeBarge (pseudonym for Etterlene Jordan)
Famous Music, 2002/Jobete Music, 2002/Pookietoots Publishing,
   2002/DJ Irv Publishing, 2002/Ensign Music, 2002
Performed by Ashanti on the album *Ashanti* (Universal, 2002).
   Nominated for a Grammy Award, Best Female R&B Vocal
   Performance, 2002.

For You
Words and music by John April, Aaron Lewis, Michael Mushok, and
   Jonathan Wysocki
Greenfund, 2001/I'm Nobody Music, 2001/My Blue Car Music, 2001/
   Pimp Yug, 2001/WB Music, 2001
Performed by Staind on the album *Break the Cycle* (Flip/Elektra, 2001).

Forgive
Words and music by Rebecca Howard and Trey Bruce
Big Red Tractor Music, 2002/EMI-April Music, 2002/Ice Trey Music,
   2002/Tennessee Colonel, 2002
Performed by Rebecca Lynn Howard on the soundtrack album
   Providence (MCA, 2002). Also included on Howard's album *Forgive*
   (MCA, 2002).

Forty Five, see **45.**

45, also known as **Forty Five**
Words and music by Elvis Costello (pseudonym for Declan MacManus)
BMG Songs, 2002
Performed by Elvis Costello on the album *When I Was Cruel* (Island,
   2002). Nominated for a Grammy Award, Best Male Rock Vocal
   Performance, 2002.

Fragile
Words and music by Sting (pseudonym for Gordon Sumner)

Magnetic Publishing (PRS), 1987/EMI-Blackwood Music, 1987
Performed by Sting on the album . . . *All This Time* (A&M, 2001). Song
  originally appeared on the album . . . *Nothing Like the Sun* (A&M,
  1987). Nominated for a Grammy Award, Best Male Pop Vocal
  Performance, 2002.

Freelove
Words and music by Martin Gore
EMI-Blackwood Music, 2001/EMI Music Publishing Ltd., 2001/
  Grabbing Hands Music, 2001
Performed by Depeche Mode on the album *Exciter* (Mute/Reprise,
  2001).

Full Moon
Words and music by Mike City (pseudonym for Michael Flowers)
Mike City Music, 2001/Warner-Tamerlane Publishing, 2001
Performed by Brandy on the album *Full Moon* (Atlantic, 2002).

Funny, also known as **Funny You Should Call Today**
Words and music by Randall Bowland, Flemuel Brown, Gerald Levert,
  and Niles McKinney
Smoobie Music, 2002/Divided Music, 2002/Rat Eater Music, 2002/
  Universal Songs of Polygram Intntl., 2002
Performed by Gerald Levert on the soundtrack album *The Transporter*
  (Elektra, 2001). Also appears on Levert's album *The G-Spot* (Elektra,
  2002).

Funny You Should Call Today, see **Funny**.

G

The Game of Love
Words and music by Gregory Alexander and Richard Nowels
EMI-April Music, 2002/Future Furniture, 2002/Keepin It Real How Bout You Music, 2002
Performed by Santana featuring Michelle Branch on the album *Shaman* (Arista, 2002). Won a Grammy Award for Best Pop Collaboration With Vocals, 2002.

Gangsta Lovin'
Words and music by Jonah Ellis, Lonnie Simmons, and Alisa Yarbrough
Taking Care of Business Music, London, England, 2002
Performed by Eve featuring Alicia Keys on the album *Eve-Olution* (Interscope, 2002).

Get Away
Words and music by Guy Courturier, Ludovic Kohler, and William Martin
Earsnot Music, 2002/WB Music, 2002
Performed by Earshot on the album *Letting Go* (Warner Bros., 2002).

Get Free
Words and music by Craig Nicholls
Ivy League Music, 2001/Mushroom Music, 2001
Performed by the Vines on the album *Highly Evolved* (Capitol, 2002).

Get Here
Words and music by Brenda Russell
Rutland Road Music, 1984/WB Music, 1984
Covered by Justin Guarini on the album *Totally Hits 2002: More Platinum Hits* (Warner Strategic, 2002). Originally performed by Brenda Russell on the album *Brenda Russell* (A&M, 1988).

Get Inside
Words and music by Shawn Economacki, Joel Ekman, Joshua Rand, and Corey Taylor

EMI-April Music, 2002/Music That Music, 2002
Performed by Stone Sour on the album *Stone Sour* (Roadrunner, 2002).
    Nominated for a Grammy Award, Best Metal Performance, 2002.

Get Mo, also known as **Get Money**
Words and music by James Watkins
Headquarters Records, 2002
Performed by Sherm Smoke featuring Bigga Figgas on the album *Sherm Smoke* (Dean's List, 2001).

Get Money, see **Get Mo**.

Get the Party Started
Words and music by Linda Perry
Famous Music, 2001/Stuck in the Throat, 2001
Performed by Pink on the album *M!ssundaztood* (Arista, 2001).
    Nominated for a Grammy Award, Best Female Pop Vocal
    Performance, 2002.

Gettin' Grown
Words and music by Cee-Lo (pseudonym for Thomas Callaway)
God Given Music, 2002
Performed by Cee-lo on the album *Cee-Lo Green and His Perfect Imperfections* (Arista, 2002). Nominated for a Grammy Award, Best Urban/Alternative Performance, 2002.

Gimme the Light
Words and music by Sean Paul (pseudonym for Sean Henriquez) and Troy Rami
Black Shadow Records, 2002/EMI-April Music, 2002
Performed by Sean Paul on the album *Dutty Rock* (VP, 2002).

Girl All the Bad Guys Want
Words and music by Jaret Reddick and Bradley Walker
Drop Your Pants Publishing, 2002/Zomba Enterprises, 2002/Sonotrock Music, 2002
Performed by Bowling for Soup on the album *Drunk Enough to Dance* (Jive, 2002). Nominated for a Grammy Award, Best Pop Performance by a Duo or Group With Vocal, 2002.

Girl Talk
Words and music by Kandi Burruss, Edmund Clement, Anita McCloud, Lisa Lopes, and T-Boz (pseudonym for Tionne Watkins)
Air Control Music, 2002/EMI-April Music, 2002/Grunge Girl Music, 2002/Kandacy Music, 2002/Butterman Land Publishing, 2002/Elsie Louise Pitts Music, 2002/Smooth C Publishing, 2002/Songs of Universal, 2002/Songs of Windswept Pacific, 2002
Performed by TLC on the album *3D* (La Face, 2002). Nominated for a

Grammy Award, Best R&B Performance by a Duo or Group With Vocal, 2002.

Girlfriend
Words and music by Charles Hugo, Justin Timberlake, and Pharrell Williams
EMI-Blackwood Music, 2001/Waters of Nazareth Publishing, 2001/ Chase Chad Music, 2001/EMI-April Music, 2001/Tennman Tunes, 2001
Performed by *NSYNC on the album *Celebrity* (Jive, 2001). Nominated for a Grammy Award, Best Pop Performance by a Duo or Group With Vocal, 2002.

Girls of Summer
Words and music by Steven Tyler (pseudonym for Steven Tallarico), Joe Perry, and Martin Frederiksen
Sony ATV Songs LLC, 2002/White Pearl Songs, 2002/Demon of Screamin Music, 2002/JuJu Rhythms, 2002
Performed by Aerosmith on the album *O Yeah!Ultimate Aerosmith Hits* (Columbia, 2002). Nominated for a Grammy Award, Best Rock Performance by a Duo or Group With Vocal, 2002.

Give My Love to Rose
Words and music by John Cash
House of Cash, 1957
Performed by Johnny Cash on the album *American IV: The Man Comes Around* (Universal, 2002). First released on Cash's album *All Aboard the Blue Train* (Sun, 1962). Won a Grammy Award for Best Male Country Vocal Performance, 2002.

Gnawin' on It
Words and music by Bonnie Raitt and Roy Rogers
Open Secret Music, Los Angeles, 2002/Chops Not Chaps Music, 2002
Performed by Bonnie Raitt on the album *Silver Lining* (Capitol, 2002). Nominated for a Grammy Award, Best Female Rock Vocal Performance, 2002.

God Bless America
Words and music by Irving Berlin
Irving Berlin Music, 1938
Covered by LeAnn Rimes on the album *God Bless America* (Curb, 2001). Also included on Rimes' album *You Light Up My Life: Inspirational Songs* (Curb, 1997). Originally performed by Kate Smith.

God Bless the U.S.A.
Words and music by Lee Greenwood
Songs of Universal, 1984/Universal Songs of Polygram Intntl., 1984

Performed by Lee Greenwood. Released as a single (Curb, 2001).
  Originally appeared on Greenwood's album *You've Got a Good Love
  Comin'* (MCA, 1985).

Goddess of Love
Words and music by Bryan Ferry and Dave Stewart
Careers-BMG Music Publishing, 2002/EMI-Virgin Songs, 2002/Bryan
  Ferry Publishing Designee (PRS), 2002/Eligible Music (PRS), 2002
Performed by Bryan Ferry on the album *Frantic* (Virgin, 2002).

The Golden Age
Words and music by Beck (pseudonym for Beck Hansen)
BMG Songs, 2002/Cyanide Breathmint Music, 2002
Performed by Beck on the album *Sea Change* (DGC, 2002).

Good Man
Words and music by India. Arie (pseudonym for India Simpson), Willie
  Baker, Maxwell Ransey, and Shannon Sanders
Berns II Music Publishing, 2002/Songs of Windswept Pacific, 2002/
  Gold and Iron Music Publishing, 2002/WB Music, 2002/Wangout,
  2002/Sony ATV Tunes LLC, 2002/Key 2 My Heart Publishing, 2002/
  Wonposet Songs, 2002
Performed by India.Arie on the album *Voyage to India* (Universal,
  2002). Nominated for a Grammy Award, Best R&B Song, 2002.

Good Morning Aztlan
Words and music by David Hidalgo and Louis Perez
Bug Music, 2002/Davince Music, 2002/No KO Music, 2002
Performed by Los Lobos on the album *Good Morning Aztlan*
  (Mammoth, 2002).

Good Morning Beautiful
Words and music by Todd Cerney and Zachary Lyle
Life of the Record Music, 2000/Mighty Moe Music, 2000/Sevens
  International, 2000
Performed by Steve Holy on the soundtrack album *Angel Eyes* (Curb,
  2001). Previously performed by Holy on the album *Blue Moon* (Curb,
  2000).

The Good Stuff
Words and music by Craig Wiseman and Jim Collins
Make Shift Music, 2002/Warner-Tamerlane Publishing, 2002/BMG
  Songs, 2002/Mrs. Lumpkin's Poodle, 2002
Performed by Kenny Chesney on the album *No Shoes, No Shirt, No
  Problems* (BNA, 2002).

Good Times
Words and music by Robert Hankerson, Marilyn McLeon, Pamela
  Sawyer, and David Styles

EMI-April Music, 2002/Jobete Music, 2002/Justin Combs Publishing, 2002/Paniro's Publishing, 2002/Denson Filez Music, 2002
Performed by Styles on the album *Gangster and a Gentleman* (Ruff Ryders, 2002).

Goodbye to You
Words and music by Michelle Branch
I'm With the Band Music, 2001/WB Music, 2001
Performed by Michelle Branch on the album *The Spirit Room* (Maverick, 2001).

Gorillaz on My Mind
Words and music by Damon Albarn, Jamie Hewlett, and Reggie Noble
Funky Noble Productions, 2002/WB Music, 2002/EMI-Blackwood Music, 2002
Performed by Redman featuring Gorillaz on the soundtrack album *Blade II* (Virgin, 2002).

Gossip Folks
Words and music by Melissa Elliott, William Bloom, Ludacris (pseudonym for Christopher Bridges), Timbaland (pseudonym for Timothy Mosley), and Franklyn Smith
EMI-April Music, 2002/Ludacris Music Publishing, 2002/Mass Confusion Productions, 2002/Virginia Beach Music, 2002/WB Music, 2002
Performed by Missy Elliott featuring Ludacris on the album *Under Construction* (Elektra, 2002).

Got Ur Self a. . .
Words and music by John Black, Howlin' Wolf (pseudonym for Chester Burnett), Simon Edwards, Nas (pseudonym for Nasir Jones), Piers Marsh, Robert Spragg, and Megahertz (pseudonym for Dorsey Wesley)
Chrysalis Music, 2001/Dors-D Music, 2001/ARC Music, 2001
Performed by Nas on the album *Stillmatic* (Ill Will, 2001).

Gots ta Be, also known as **Gotta Be**
Words and music by Mischke Butler, Harvey Mason, Steven Russell, and Damon Thomas
BMG Songs, 2002/Demis Hot Songs, 2002/E Two Music, 2002/EMI-April Music, 2002/Mischkemusic, 2002/Music of Windswept, 2002/Strange Motel Music, 2002
Performed by B2K on the album *B2K* (Epic, 2002).

Gotta Be, see **Gots ta Be**.

Gotta Get Thru This
Words and music by Daniel Bedingfield
Reverb America Music, London, England, 2002/Songs of Universal,

2002
Performed by Daniel Bedingfield on the album *Gotta Get Thru This*
(Universal, 2002). Nominated for a Grammy Award, Best Dance
Recording, 2002.

Grindin'

Words and music by Sean Paul (pseudonym for Sean Henriquez),
Charles Hugo, Malice (pseudonym for Gene Thornton), Pusha T
(pseudonym for Terrence Thornton), and Pharrell Williams
Chase Chad Music, 2002/Dutty Rock Music, 2002/EMI-April Music,
2002/Gemarc, 2002/Terrardome Music, 2002/EMI-Blackwood Music,
2002/Waters of Nazareth Publishing, 2002
Performed by Clipse on the album *Lord Willin'* (Arista, 2002).

H

Hailee's Song
Words and music by Eminem (pseudonym for Marshall Mathers) and Luis Resto
Eight Mile Style Music, 2002/Ensign Music, 2002/Restaurant's World Music, 2002
Performed by Eminem on the album *The Eminem Show* (Interscope, 2002).

Halfcrazy
Words and music by Ivan Barias, Carvin Haggins, Musiq (pseudonym for Talib Johnson), and Francis Lai
EMI-April Music, 2002/Nivrac Tyke Music, 2002/Soul Child Music, 2002/Tetragrammaton Music, 2002/Touched by Jazz Music, 2002/ Universal Music Publishing, 2002/EMI Unart Catalogue, 2002
Performed by Musiq on the album *Juslisen* (Def Soul, 2002). Nominated for a Grammy Award, Best Male R&B Vocal Performance, 2002.

Hands Clean
Words and music by Alanis Morissette
1974 Music, 2002/Universal-MCA Music Publishing, 2002
Performed by Alanis Morissette on the album *Under Rug Swept* (Maverick, 2002). Also included on Morissette's album *Feast on Scraps* (Maverick, 2002).

The Hands That Built America
Words and music by Bono (pseudonym for Paul Hewson), The Edge (pseudonym for David Evans), Adam Clayton, and Larry Mullen, Jr
Universal Polygram International Pub., 2002
Performed by U2 in the film and on the soundtrack album *Gangs of New York* (Interscope, 2002). Also included on U2's album *The Best of 1990-2000* (Interscope, 2002). Nominated for an Academy Award, Best Original Song, 2002.

Happy
Words and music by Andre Parker, Raymond Calhoun, Ashanti

Douglas, and Irv Gotti (pseudonym for Irving Lorenzo)
Taking Care of Business Music, London, England, 2002/Famous Music,
   2002/Pookietoots Publishing, 2002/Soldierz Touch, 2002/DJ Irv
   Publishing, 2002/Ensign Music, 2002
Performed by Ashanti on the album *Ashanti* (Murder Inc., 2002).

Hate to Say I Told You So
Words and music by Randy Fitzsimmons
WB Music, 2000
Performed by the Hives on the soundtrack album *Spider-Man*
   (Columbia, 2002). Originally appeared on the Hives' album *Veni Vidi
   Vicious* (Burning Heart, 2000).

Hazard to Myself, see Don't Let Me Get Me.

He Loves Me (Lyzel in E Flat) (Movements I, II, III)
Words by Jill Scott, music by Keith Pelzer
Blue's Baby Music, 2000/EMI-April Music, 2000/Jay Qui Music, 2000/
   Touched by Jazz Music, 2000
Performed by Jill Scott on the album *Experience: Jill Scott 826+* (Sony,
   2001). Originally appeared on *Who Is Jill Scott?: Words and Sounds,
   Vol. 1* (Hidden Beach, 2000). Nominated for a Grammy Award, Best
   Female R&B Vocal Performance, 2002.

He Think I Don't Know
Words and music by Gerald Isaac
Careers-BMG Music Publishing, 2002/Hollow Thigh Music, 2002
Performed by Mary J. Blige featuring Common on the album *No More
   Drama* (MCA, 2002). Also appears on Blige's album *Dance for Me*
   (MCA, 2002). Won a Grammy Award for Best Female R&B Vocal
   Performance, 2002.

Head on Collision
Words and music by Chad Gilbert, Cyrus Bolooki, Ian Grushka, Jordan
   Pundik, and Stephen Klein
Blanco Meow Music, 2002/Universal Tunes, 2002
Performed by New Found Glory on the album *Sticks and Stones* (MCA,
   2002).

Headstrong
Words and music by Christopher Brown, Kurt Charell, and Simon
   Ormandy
Traptism, 2002/W B M Music, 2002
Performed by Trapt on the album *Trapt* (Warner Bros., 2002).

Hearts of Stone
Words and music by David Hidalgo and Louis Perez
Bug Music, 2002/Davince Music, 2002/No KO Music, 2002

Performed by Los Lobos on the album *Good Morning Aztlan* (Mammoth, 2002).

Heathen (The Rays)
Words and music by David Bowie (pseudonym for David Jones)
Nipple Music, 2002
Performed by David Bowie on the album *Heathen* (ISO/Columbia, 2002).

Heaven
Words and music by Bryan Adams and James Vallance
Almo Music, 1983/Testatyme Music, 1983/Irving Music, 1983
Covered by DJ Sammy featuring Yanou and Do on the album *Heaven* (Robbins, 2002). Originally performed by Bryan Adams on the album*Reckless* (A&M, 1984).

Heaven I Need a Hug
Words and music by R. Kelly (pseudonym for Steven Williams)
R. Kelly Music, 2002/Zomba Songs, 2002
Performed by R. Kelly. Released as a single (Jive, 2002).

Hella Good
Words and music by Charles Hugo, Gwen Stefani, Pharrell Williams, and Tony Kanal
Chase Chad Music, 2002/EMI-April Music, 2002/Universal-MCA Music Publishing, 2002/EMI-Blackwood Music, 2002/Waters of Nazareth Publishing, 2002
Performed by No Doubt on the album *Rock Steady* (Interscope, 2001). Nominated for a Grammy Award, Best Dance Recording, 2002.

Help Me
Words and music by Matthew Gerrard and Michele Vice-Maslin
G Matt Music, 2002/WB Music, 2002/More Sweeter Songs, 2002
Performed by Nick Carter on the album *Now or Never* (Jive, 2002).

Here I Am
Words and music by Bryan Adams, Gretchen Daniel, and Hans Zimmer
2855 Music, 2002/SKG Music Publishing, 2002/Zomba Enterprises, 2002
Performed by Bryan Adams on the soundtrack album *Spirit: Stallion of the Cimarron* (Universal, 2002).

Here Is Gone
Words and music by John Rzeznik
Corner of Clark and Kent, 2002/EMI-Virgin Music, 2002
Performed by Goo Goo Dolls on the album *Gutterflower* (Warner Bros., 2002).

Here to Stay
Words and music by Fieldy (pseudonym for Reginald Arvizu), Jonathan
    Davis, James Shaffer, David Silveria, and Brian Welch
Evileria Music, 2002/Fieldysnuttz Music, 2002/Gintoe Music, 2002/
    Musik Munk Publishing, 2002/Stratosphericyoness Music, 2002/
    Zomba Songs, 2002
Performed by Korn on the album *Untouchables* (Epic, 2002). Won a
    Grammy Award for Best Metal Performance, 2002.

Hero
Words and music by Chad Kroeger
Warner-Tamerlane Publishing, 2002/Arm Your Dillo, 2002
Performed by Chad Kroeger featuring Josey Scott on the soundtrack
    album *Spider-Man* (Columbia/Roadrunner/Island Def Jam/Sony Music
    Soundtrax, 2002). Nominated for Grammy Awards, Best Rock
    Performance by a Duo or Group With Vocal, 2002, Best Rock Song,
    2002, and Best Song Written for a Motion Picture/Television, 2002.

Hey Baby
Words and music by Gwen Stefani, Thomas Dumont, Tony Kanal, and
    Bounty Killer (pseudonym for Rodney Price)
Universal-MCA Music Publishing, 2001/World of the Dolphin Music,
    2001
Performed by No Doubt on the album *Rock Steady* (Interscope, 2001).
    Won a Grammy Award for Best Pop Performance by a Duo or Group
    With Vocal, 2002.

Hey Ma
Words and music by Cameron Giles, Darryl Pittman, and Lionel Richie
Jobete Music, 2002/Libren Music, 2002/Next Level Groove Music,
    2002/Killa Cam Music, 2002
Performed by Cam'ron featuring Juelz Santana and Freekey on the
    album *Come Home With Me* (Roc-a-Fella, 2002).

Hey Sexy Lady
Words and music by Shaggy (pseudonym for Orville Burrell),
    Christopher Circh, Richardo Ducent, Robert Livingston, Patrick
    Morrison, and Brian Thompson
Livingsting Music, 2002/WB Music, 2002
Performed by Shaggy on the album *Lucky Day* (MCA, 2002).

The Hindu Times
Words and music by Noel Gallagher
Sony ATV Songs LLC, 2002
Performed by Oasis on the album *Heathen Chemistry* (Epic, 2002).

Hip-Hop
Words and music by Easy Mo Bee (pseudonym for Osten Harvey) and

Afu-Ra (pseudonym for Aaron Phillip)
Life Force Music, 2001/Bee Mo Easy Music, 2001/EMI-April Music, 2001
Performed by Afu-Ra on the album *Life Force Radio* (Koch International, 2002).

Hit Somebody! (The Hockey Song)
Words and music by Warren Zevon and Mitch Albom
Zevon Music, 2001/Mitch Albom Music, 2001
Performed by Warren Zevon on the album *My Ride's Here* (Artemis, 2002).

Hold Me Down
Words and music by Tommy Lee (pseudonym for Thomas Lee Bass) and Kai Huppenen
Gimme Back My Publishing, 2002
Performed by Tommy Lee on the album *Never a Dull Moment* (MCA, 2002).

Hot in Herre
Words by Nelly (pseudonym for Cornell Haynes) and Charles Brown, music by Pharrell Williams
BMG Music Publishing Ltd., 2002/Ascent Music Inc., 2002/EMI-Blackwood Music, 2002/Nouveaux Music, 2002/Swing T Publishing, 2002/Waters of Nazareth Publishing, 2002/Jackie Frost Music, 2002
Performed by Nelly on the album *Nellyville* (Universal, 2002). Won a Grammy Award for Best Male Rap Solo Performance, 2002.

How You Remind Me
Words and music by Chad Kroeger, music by Michael Kroeger, Ryan Peake, and Ryan Vikedal
Warner-Tamerlane Publishing, 2001
Performed by Nickelback on the album *Silver Side Up* (Roadrunner, 2001). Nominated for a Grammy Award, Record of the Year, 2002.

Hush Lil' Baby, see Hush Lil' Lady.

Hush Lil' Lady, also known as Hush Lil' Baby
Words and music by Shari Gray, Corey Hodges, Marcus Lee, Dwayne Smalls, and Sean Smith
It Was Written Publishing, 2001/Christopher Matthew Music, 2001/Hitco Music, 2001
Performed by Corey with Lil' Romeo and Lil' Reema on the album *I'm Just Corey* (Motown, 2002).

I

I Am Mine
Words and music by Eddie Vedder
Innocent Bystander Music, 2002
Performed by Pearl Jam on the album *Riot Act* (Epic, 2002).

I Am Trying to Break Your Heart
Words and music by Jeff Tweedy
Words Ampersand Music, 2002
Performed by Wilco on the album *Yankee Hotel Foxtrot* (Nonesuch, 2002).

I Breathe In, I Breathe Out
Words and music by Christopher Cagle and Jon Robbin
Sony ATV Tunes LLC, 1998/Ten Ten Tunes, 1998
Performed by Chris Cagle on the album *Play It Loud* (Capitol, 2001).
    Originally performed by David Kersh on the album *If I Never Stop Loving You* (Curb, 1998).

I Care 4 U
Words and music by Melissa Elliott and Timbaland (pseudonym for Timothy Mosley)
Mass Confusion Productions, 2001/Virginia Beach Music, 2001
Performed by Aaliyah on the album *I Care 4 U* (Blackground, 2002).
    Originally performed by Aaliyah on the album *Aaliyah* (Blackground, 2001).

I Don't Have to Be Me ('Til Monday)
Words and music by Steve Azar, Dan Shipley, and Jason Young
Careers-BMG Music Publishing, 2002/Mas Venture Music, 2002/ Misterssippi Music, 2002
Performed by Steve Azar on the album *Waitin' on Joe* (Mercury, 2002).

I Don't Want You to Go
Words and music by Carolyn Johnson and William Polk
April Blue Music, 1999/Blakemore Avenue Music, 1999/EMI-Full Keel

Music, 1999/Songs of Mosaic, 1999/Songs of Otis Barker, 1999
Performed by Carolyn Dawn Johnson on the album *Room With a View*
(Arista, 2001).

I Just Wanna Be Mad
Words and music by Kelley Lovelace and Lee Miller
Hold Jack Music, 2002/Mosaic Music, 2002/EMI-April Music, 2002
Performed by Terri Clark. Released as a single (Mercury, 2002).

I Keep Looking
Words and music by Sara Evans, Anthony Martin, and Tom Shapiro
Mosaic Music, 2000/Sony ATV Songs LLC, 2000/Sony ATV Tree
Publishing, 2000/Wenonga Music, 2000
Performed by Sara Evans on the album *Born to Fly* (RCA, 2002).

I Love You
Words and music by Anthony Best, Faith Evans, Isaac Hayes, Mechalie
Jamison, Jennifer Lopez, Bobby Springsteen, and Mario Winans
Chyna Baby Music, 2002/Cori Tiffani Publishing, 2002/EMI-Blackwood
Music, 2002/Incense Productions, 2002/Janice Combs Music, 2002/
Marsky Music, 2002/Sony ATV Songs LLC, 2002/Universal Duchess
Music, 2002/B Springs Publishing, 2002/BMG Songs, 2002/EMI-
April Music, 2002/Gloria's Boy Music, 2002/Justin Combs
Publishing, 2002
Performed by Faith Evans on the album *Faithfully* (Bad Boy, 2002).

I Miss My Friend
Words and music by Anthony Martin, Mark Nesler, and Tom Shapiro
Buna Boy Music, 2000/Glitterfish Music, 2000/Mosaic Music, 2000/
Sony ATV Tree Publishing, 2000/Wenonga Music, 2000
Performed by Darryl Worley on the album *I Miss My Friend*
(DreamWorks, 2002).

I Move On
Words by Fred Ebb, music by John Kander
Kander & Ebb, 1975/Unichappell Music Inc., 1975
Performed by Catherine Zeta-Jones and Renee Zellweger on the
soundtrack album *Chicago* (Epic/Sony Music Soundtrax, 2002).
Nominated for an Academy Award, Best Original Song, 2002.

I Need a Girl (Part One)
Words and music by Chauncey Hawkins, Knight Jack, Michael Jones,
Eric Matlock, and Tijuan Frampton
Coptic Soundsations Publishing, 2002/Dakoda House, 2002/Donceno
Music Publishing, 2002/EMI-April Music, 2002/Hot Heat Music,
2002/Justin Combs Publishing, 2002
Performed by P. Diddy featuring Usher and Loon on the album *We
Invented the Remix* (Bad Boy, 2002).

I Need a Girl (Part Two)

Words and music by P. Diddy (pseudonym for Sean Combs), Chauncey Hawkins, Michael Jones, Frankie Romano, Taurian Shropshire, and Mario Winans

EMI-Blackwood Music, 2002/Janice Combs Music, 2002/Marsky Music, 2002/Donceno Music Publishing, 2002/EMI-April Music, 2002/Hot Heat Music, 2002/Jessy Jaye Music, 2002/Justin Combs Publishing, 2002

Performed by P. Diddy featuring Ginuwine, Loon, Mario Winans and Tammy Ruggeri on the album *We Invented the Remix* (Bad Boy, 2002).

I Need You

Words and music by Mark Rooney

Cori Tiffani Publishing, 2001/Sony ATV Songs LLC, 2001

Performed by Marc Anthony on the album *Mended* (Columbia, 2001).

I Should Be Sleeping

Words and music by Lisa Drew and Charlotte Smith

EMI-April Music, 2002/Jersey Girl Music, 2002/EMI-Blackwood Music, 2002/Zomba Songs, 2002

Performed by Emerson Drive on the album *Emerson Drive* (DreamWorks, 2002).

I Stand Alone

Words and music by Salvatore Erna

Meeengya Music, 2002/Universal-MCA Music Publishing, 2002

Performed by Godsmack on the soundtrack album *The Scorpion King* (Universal, 2002). Nominated for Grammy Awards, Best Hard Rock Performance, 2002, and Best Rock Song, 2002.

I Thought I Told You That

Words and music by Nicole Harris, Malek Milkos, and Anastacia Newkirk

Melodious Fool Music, 2001/Po Ho Productions, 2001/Universal Music Publishing, 2001/WB Music, 2001

Performed by Anastacia featuring Faith Evans on the album *Freak of Nature* (Epic, 2001)

I Want to Be Your Mother's Son-in-Law

Words and music by Mann Holiner and Alberta Nichols

Anne-Rachel Music, 1933

Covered by Macy Gray on the soundtrack album *Divine Secrets of the Ya-Ya Sisterhood* (DMZ/Columbia, 2002). Originally performed by Benny Goodman & His Orchestra featuring Billie Holiday.

I Will Be Heard

Words and music by James Shanahan

800 Pound Gorilla Music, 2002
Performed by Hatebreed on the soundtrack album *XXX* (Universal, 2002). Also appears on Hatebreed's album *Perseverance* (Stillborn/Republic/Universal, 2002).

I Wish I Didn't Miss You Anymore, see **Wish I Didn't Miss You**.

If I Could Go!
Words and music by Jamar Austin, Cynthia Loving, Angie Martinez, and Ricardo Thomas
Mo Loving Music, 2002/Angie Martinez Music, 2002/Cyphercleff Music Publishing, 2002
Performed by Angie Martinez featuring Lil' Mo and Sacario on the album *Animal House* (Elektra, 2002).

If I Didn't Have You
Words and music by Randy Newman
Walt Disney Music Co., 2001
Performed by Randy Newman on the soundtrack album *Monsters, Inc.* (Disney, 2001). Won a Grammy Award for Best Song Written for a Motion Picture/Television, 2002.

If We Could Remember
Words and music by Jerrald Goldsmith and Paul Williams
Ensign Music, 2001/Famous Music, 2001/Hillabeans Music, 2001
Performed by Yolanda Adams on the soundtrack album *The Sum of All Fears* (Elektra, 2002).

I'll Take the Rain
Words and music by Peter Buck, Michael Mills, and Michael Stipe
Temporary Music, 2001
Performed by R.E.M. on the album *Reveal* (Warner Bros., 2001).

I'm Alive
Words and music by Andreas Carlsson and Kristian Lundin
WB Music, 2002
Performed by Celine Dion on the album *A New Day Has Come* (Epic, 2002).

I'm Gonna Be Alright
Words and music by Jennifer Lopez, Cadillac Tah (pseudonym for Cory Rooney), Troy Oliver, Lorraine Cook, Ronald Lapread, A. Hill, M. Thompson, and M. Marshall, music by Jean Claude Oliver and Samuel Barnes
Nuyorican Publishing, 2002/Sony ATV Songs LLC, 2002/Cori Tiffani Publishing, 2002/Sony ATV Tunes LLC, 2002/Milk Chocolate Factory, 2002/EMI-April Music, 2002/Danica Music, 2002/Lehsem Songs, 2002

Jennifer Lopez featuring 50 Cent on the album *J to Tha L-O!: The Remixes* (Epic, 2002).

I'm Gonna Getcha Good!
Words and music by Shania Twain (pseudonym for Eilleen Regina Lange) and Robert Lange
Loon Echo Music, 2002/Universal Songs of Polygram Intntl., 2002/ Universal Polygram International Pub., 2002/Zomba Enterprises, 2002
Performed by Shania Twain on the album *Up!* (Universal, 2002).

I'm Gonna Miss Her, also known as Fishin' Song
Words and music by Brad Paisley and Frank Rogers
EMI-April Music, 2001/Sea Gayle Music, 2001
Performed by Brad Paisley on the album *Part II* (Arista, 2001). Nominated for a Grammy Award, Best Male Country Vocal Performance, 2002.

I'm Not a Girl, Not Yet a Woman
Words and music by Dido (pseudonym for Dido Armstrong), Max Martin (pseudonym for Martin Sandberg), and Rami (pseudonym for Rami Yacoub)
WB Music, 2001/Zomba Enterprises, 2001
Performed by Britney Spears on the album *Britney* (Jive, 2001).

I'm Still Standing
Words and music by Helsa Ariass and Eartha Moore
AFRT Music, 2002/Serrano 105 Publishing, 2002
Performed by Eartha on the album *Sidebars* (AFRT, 2002). Nominated for a Grammy Award, Best Female R&B Vocal Performance, 2002.

The Impossible
Words and music by John Lovelace and Lee Miller
EMI-April Music, 2002/Mosaic Music, 2002
Performed by Joe Nichols on the album *Man With a Memory* (Universal, 2002). Nominated for Grammy Awards, Best Country Song, 2002, and Best Male Country Vocal Performance, 2002.

In My Place
Words and music by Guy Berryman, Jonathan Buckland, William Champion, and Christopher Martin
BMG Songs, 2002
Performed by Coldplay on the album *A Rush of Blood to the Head* (Capitol, 2002). Won a Grammy Award for Best Rock Performance by a Duo or Group With Vocal, 2002.

Innervision
Words by Serj Tankian, music by Daron Malakian
Sony ATV Tunes LLC, 2002/Ddevil Music, 2002

Performed by System of a Down on the album *Steal This Album!* (American/Columbia, 2002).

It's Gonna Be. . . (A Lovely Day)
Words and music by Bruce Aisher, Luke Brancaccio, Thomas Digweed, Nick Muir, Skip Scarborough, and Bill Withers
Unichappell Music Inc., 2002
Performed by Brancaccio and Aisher. Released as a single (Nettwerk, 2002).

It's a Good Life If You Don't Weaken
Words and music by Robert Baker, Gordon Downie, John Fay, Paul Langlois, and Robert Sinclair
Arte Humane, 2002/Bhaji Maker, 2002/Ching Music, 2002/Dirty Shorts, 2002/Wiener Art, 2002/Songs of Peer, 2002
Performed by the Tragically Hip on the album *In Violet Light* (Zoe/Rounder 2002).

It's Love (Trippin')
Words and music by Darren Henson, Keith Pelzer, and Jill Scott
Blue's Baby Music, 2002/EMI-April Music, 2002/Jat Cat Music Publishing, 2002/Jay Qui Music, 2002/No Gravity Music, 2002/Touched by Jazz Music, 2002
Performed by Andrea Brown. Released as a single (Strictly Rhythm, 2002).

It's Not Fair
Words and music by Vidal Davis, Andre Harris, and Glenn Lewis (pseudonym for Glenn Ricketts)
Dirty Dre Music, 2002/EMI-April Music, 2002/Jat Cat Music Publishing, 2002/Touched by Jazz Music, 2002/Universal Music Publishing, 2002/WB Music, 2002
Performed by Glenn Lewis on the album *World Outside My Window* (Epic, 2002).

It's So Easy
Words and music by Sheryl Crow and Kathryn Crow
Old Crow Music, 2002/Warner-Tamerlane Publishing, 2002/Young Crow Music, 2002
Performed by Sheryl Crow featuring Don Henley on the album *c'mon, c'mon* (A&M, 2002). Nominated for a Grammy Award, Best Pop Collaboration With Vocals, 2002.

It's the Weekend
Words and music by Kandi Burruss, Anthony Harris, La Marquis Jefferson, Shannon Johnson, and Jermaine Dupri (pseudonym for Jermaine Mauldin)
Notting Hill Music, London, England, 2001/Air Control Music, 2001/

EMI-April Music, 2001/Kandacy Music, 2001/Me and Marq Music, 2001/So So Def Music, 2001

Performed by Lil' J on the soundtrack album *Clockstoppers* (Hollywood, 2002). Originally appeared on Lil' J's album *All About J* (Hollywood, 2001).

I've Got You

Words and music by Kara Dioguardi and Cadillac Tah (pseudonym for Cory Rooney)

Cori Tiffani Publishing, 2001/K Stuff Publishing, 2001/Sony ATV Songs LLC, 2001

Performed by Marc Anthony on the album *Mended* (Columbia, 2001).

J

Jenny from the Block
Words and music by Miro Arbex, Samuel Barnes, Andre Deyo, Jennifer
Lopez, Michael Oliver, Troy Oliver, Jean Claude Oliver, Lawrence
Parker, and Scott Sterling
Nuyorican Publishing, 2002/Sony ATV Songs LLC, 2002/Sony ATV
Tunes LLC, 2002/Milk Chocolate Factory, 2002/Ekop Publishing,
2002/Enot Publishing, 2002/Tunesmith Advancements, 2002/Jaedon
Christopher Publishing, 2002/EMI-April Music, 2002/N Key Music,
2002/Paniro's Publishing, 2002
Performed by Jennifer Lopez featuring Jadakiss and Styles on the album
This Is Me. . . Then (Epic, 2002).

Joe Fabulous
Words and music by Paul Rodgers
Ramshackle Music, 2002
Performed by Bad Company on the album *In Concert: Merchants of
Cool* (Sanctuary, 2002).

John Walker's Blues
Words and music by Steve Earle
Sarangel Music, 2002
Performed by Steve Earle on the album *Jerusalem* (E-Squared/Artemis,
2002).

Just a Friend
Words and music by Warryn Campbell, Biz Markie (pseudonym for
Marcel Hall), Harold Lilly, and John Smith
EMI-Blackwood Music, 2002/Uncle Bobby Music, 2002/Cold Chillin'
Music, 2002/WB Music, 2002
Performed by Mario (J, 2002). Initially released as a single; later
featured on the album *Mario* (J, 2002). Based on the song by Biz
Markie.

Just Like a Pill
Words and music by Dallas Austin and Pink (pseudonym for Alecia

Moore)

Cryptron Music, 2001/EMI-Blackwood Music, 2001/EMI-April Music, 2001/Pink Panther Music, 2001

Performed by Pink on the album *M!ssundaztood* (Arista, 2001).

Just Rock & Roll

Words and music by Gabriel Saporta

Midtown Rock Music, 2000

Performed by Midtown on the album *Save the World, Lose the Girl* (Drive-Thru, 2000).

Just What I Do

Words and music by Brian Burns and Ira Dean

Magic Penny Music, 2001/Hapsack Music, 2001/Warner-Tamerlane Publishing, 2001

Performed by Trick Pony on the album *Trick Pony* (Warner Bros., 2001). Nominated for a Grammy Award, Best Country Performance by a Duo/Group With Vocal, 2002.

K

The Ketchup Song (Hey Hah), also known as **Asereje**
Words and music by Manuel Ruiz
Sony ATV Tunes LLC, 2001
Performed by Las Ketchup on the album *Hijas Del Tomate* (Columbia, 2002).

The Key to Gramercy Park
Words and music by Exeter Blue (pseudonym for Elijah Blue), Dr. Nner (pseudonym for Renn Hawkey), Alec Pure (pseudonym for Alec Puro), Josh Richman, Carlton Megalodon (pseudonym for Carlton Bost), and C. Riker
Sedge Music, 1999/Dreamworks Songs, 1999/LaGamorph, 1999/Cartoon Aroma Hand Music, 1999/Blue Haze Music, 1999/Craig Beast Music, 1999
Performed by Deadsy on the album *Commencement* (Elementree/DreamWorks, 1999).

Knoc
Words and music by Melissa Elliott, Knoc-Turn'al (pseudonym for Royal Harbor), Francis Palacios, Wallace Sibley, Ross Sloan, and Dr. Dre (pseudonym for Andre Young)
East New York Music, 2002/Spydox Publishing, 2002/Knoc Turn Al Music, 2002
Performed by Knoc-Turn'al featuring Dr. Dre and Missy Elliott on the album *L.A. Confidential Presents: Knoc-Turn'al* (Elektra, 2002). Nominated for a Grammy Award, Best Short Form Music Video, 2002.

L

La Negra Tiene Tumbao
Words and music by Sergio George and Fernando Ororio
Sir George Music, 2001/Fernando Osorio Songs, 2001/Warner-
 Tamerlane Publishing, 2001
Performed by Celia Cruz on the album *La Negra Tiene Tumbao* (Sony
 International, 2001).

Lady
Words and music by Thomas Hammer and Sandra St. Victor
EMI-April Music, 1999/Lonely Town Music, 1999/Maanami Music,
 1999
Covered by the Temptations on the album *Awesome* (Universal, 2001).
 Originally performed by Profyle on the album *Whispers in the Dark*
 (Motown, 1999). Nominated for a Grammy Award, Best Traditional
 R&B Vocal Performance, 2002.

Landslide
Words and music by Stevie Nicks
Welsh Witch Music, 1975
Covered by Dixie Chicks on the album *Home* (Open Wide/Monument/
 Columbia, 2002). Originally performed by Fleetwood Mac on the
 album *Fleetwood Mac* (Reprise, 1975).

The Last DJ
Words and music by Tom Petty
Adria K Music, 2002
Performed by Tom Petty & the Heartbreakers on the album *The Last DJ*
 (Warner Bros., 2002).

Lately
Words and music by Greg Brown
Hacklebarney Music, 1994
Covered by Lucinda Williams on the album *Going Driftless: An Artist's
 Tribute to Greg Brown* (Red House, 2002). Originally performed by
 Greg Brown on the album *The Poet Game* (Red House, 1994).

Nominated for a Grammy Award, Best Female Country Vocal Performance, 2002.

Let It Rain
Words and music by Robert Boyd, Wesley Clark, and John Gregson
Bobby Boyd Music, 2000/Bonedaddy's Publishing, 2000/Drippin' Publishing, 2000
Performed by W. C. Clark on the album *From Austin With Soul* (Alligator, 2002).

Let's Stay Home Tonight
Words and music by Johnta Austin, Joel Campbell, and Allen Gordon, Jr
Chrysalis Music, 2001/Daddy's Downstairs Again, 2001/Lexy's Daddy's Music, 2001/Naked Under My Clothes Music, 2001
Performed by Joe on the album *Better Days* (Jive, 2001). Nominated for a Grammy Award, Best Male R&B Vocal Performance, 2002.

Lick My Neck, see **My Neck My Back (Lick It)**.

Life Goes On
Words and music by Andreas Carlsson, Desmond Child, and LeAnn Rimes
Angel Pie Publishing, 2002/Mike Curb Music, 2002/Deston Songs, 2002/WB Music, 2002/Andreas Carlsson Publishing, 2002/Sony ATV Tunes LLC, 2002/Desmundo Music, 2002
Performed by LeAnn Rimes on the album *Twisted Angel* (Curb, 2002).

Lifestyles of the Rich and Famous
Words and music by Benjamin Madden and Joel Madden
EMI-April Music, 2002/21:1 Music, 2002
Performed by Good Charlotte on the album *Young and the Hopeless* (Epic/Daylight, 2002).

Lights, Camera, Action!
Words and music by Leonard Caston, Mr. Cheeks (pseudonym for Terrance Kelly), Anita Poree, and Frank Wilson
Stone Diamond Music, 2001/Mr. Cheeks Publishing, 2001/Universal Music Publishing, 2001
Performed by Mr. Cheeks on the album *John P. Kelly* (Uptown/Universal, 2001).

Like I Love You
Words and music by Charles Hugo, Justin Timberlake, and Pharrell Williams
EMI-Blackwood Music, 2002/Waters of Nazareth Publishing, 2002/Chase Chad Music, 2002/EMI-April Music, 2002/Tennman Tunes, 2002/Gemarc/Terrardome Music

Performed by Justin Timberlake on the album *Justified* (Jive, 2002).
Nominated for a Grammy Award, Best Rap/Sung Collaboration, 2002.

Lil' Jack Slade
Music by Emily Erwin (pseudonym for Emily Robison), Terri Hendrix,
Lloyd Maines, and Martie Seidel (pseudonym for Martie MaGuire)
Artmob Music, 2002/Bug Music, 2002/THM Music, 2002/Woolly
Puddin' Music, 2002
Performed by Dixie Chicks on the album *Home* (Open Wide/Monument/
Columbia, 2002). Won a Grammy Award for Best Country
Instrumental Performance, 2002.

A Little Less Conversation
Words and music by Mac Davis and Billy Strange
Cherry River Music, 1968/Chrysalis Songs, 1968
JXL remix from the soundtrack album *Ocean's Eleven* (Warner Bros.,
2001). Also appeared on the Elvis Presley compilation album *30 #1
Hits* (RCA, 2002). Song originally appeared on Elvis' album *Almost
In Love* (RCA Camden, 1970).

Little Things
Words and music by India. Arie (pseudonym for India Simpson), Louis
Fischer, Anthony Roberson, Sharon Sanders, and David Wolinski
Big Elk Music, 2002/Bughouse, 2002/Gold and Iron Music Publishing,
2002/Key 2 My Heart Publishing, 2002/WB Music, 2002/Universal-
MCA Music Publishing, 2002/Wangout, 2002/Sony ATV Tunes LLC,
2002
Performed by India.Arie on the album *Voyage to India* (Universal,
2002). Won a Grammy Award for Best Urban/Alternative
Performance, 2002.

Living and Living Well
Words and music by Anthony Martin, Mark Nesler, and Tom Shapiro
Buna Boy Music, 2000/Glitterfish Music, 2000/Mosaic Music, 2000/
Sony ATV Tree Publishing, 2000/Wenonga Music, 2000
Performed by George Strait on the album *The Road Less Traveled*
(MCA, 2001).

Lonesome Day
Words and music by Bruce Springsteen
Bruce Springsteen Publishing, 2002
Performed by Bruce Springsteen on the album *The Rising* (Columbia,
2002).

The Long Goodbye
Words and music by Ronan Keating and Paul Brady
WB Music, 2001/Universal Songs of Polygram Intntl., 2001
Covered by Brooks & Dunn on the album *Steers & Stripes* (Arista,

2001). Originally performed by Paul Brady on the album *Oh What a World* (Compass, 2001).

Long Time Gone
Words and music by James Darrell Scott
Chuck Wagon Gourmet Music, 2002/Famous Music, 2002
Performed by Dixie Chicks on the album *Home* (Open Wide/Monument/ Columbia, 2002). Won a Grammy Award for Best Country Performance by a Duo/Group With Vocal, 2002. Nominated for a Grammy Award, Best Country Song, 2002.

Long Way to Richmond, see **Modern Day Bonnie and Clyde**.

Lose Yourself
Words and music by Eminem (pseudonym for Marshall Mathers), Jeffrey Bass, and Luis Resto
Eight Mile Style Music, 2002
Performed by Eminem on the soundtrack album *8 Mile* (Shady/ Interscope, 2002). Won an Academy Award for Best Original Song, 2002.

Lost in Space
Words and music by Aimee Mann
Aimee Mann, 2002
Performed by Aimee Mann on the album *Lost in Space* (Superego, 2002).

A Lot of Things Different
Words and music by Bill Anderson and Dean Dillon
Mr. Bubba Music, 2002/Sony/ATV Acuff Rose Music, 2002/Sony ATV Tree Publishing, 2002
Performed by Kenny Chesney on the album *No Shoes, No Shirt, No Problems* (BNA, 2002).

Love at First Sight
Words and music by Julian Gallagher, Martin Harrington, Ashley Howes, Kylie Minogue, and Richard Stannard
Chrysalis Music, 2001/EMI-April Music, 2001/Sony Tunes, 2001/ Universal Polygram International Pub., 2001
Performed by Kylie Minogue on the album *Fever* (Capitol, 2002). Nominated for a Grammy Award, Best Dance Recording, 2002.

Love of My Life (An Ode to Hip Hop)
Words and music by Robert Ozuna, James Poyser, Common (pseudonym for Lonnie Rashid), Raphael Saadiq, Glenn Standridge, and Erykah Badu (pseudonym for Erica Wright)
BMG Songs, 2002/Divine Pimp Publishing, 2002/Jajapo Music, 2002/ Jake and the Phatman Music, 2002/TCF Music Publishing, 2002/ Ugmoe Music, 2002/Fox Film Music, 2002/Senseless Music, 2002/

Songs of Universal, 2002

Performed by Erykah Badu featuring Common on the soundtrack album *Brown Sugar* (MCA, 2002). Won a Grammy Award for Best R&B Song, 2002. Nominated for Grammy Awards, Best Song Written for a Motion Picture/Television, 2002, and Best Urban/Alternative Performance, 2002.

Love Theme from the Godfather

Music by Nino Rota

Famous Music, 1972

Covered by Slash on the soundtrack album *The Kid Stays in the Picture* (Milan, 2002). Originally performed on the soundtrack album *The Godfather* (MCA, 1972). Nominated for a Grammy Award, Best Rock Instrumental Performance, 2002.

Love's in Need of Love Today

Words and music by Stevie Wonder

Black Bull Music, 1976/Jobete Music, 1976

Performed by Stevie Wonder featuring Take Six on the album *America: A Tribute to Heroes* (Interscope, 2001). Originally performed by Wonder on the album *Songs in the Key of Life* (Motown, 1976). Won a Grammy Award for Best R&B Performance by a Duo or Group With Vocal, 2002.

Luv U Better

Words and music by Charles Hugo, LL Cool J (pseudonym for James Smith), and Pharrell Williams

Chase Chad Music, 2002/Def Jam Music, 2002/EMI-April Music, 2002/ EMI-Blackwood Music, 2002/Waters of Nazareth Publishing, 2002

Performed by LL Cool J on the album *10* (Def Jam, 2002).

M

Makin' Good Love
Words and music by Myron Avant and Stephen Huff
Grindtime Publishing, 2002/Pay Town Publishing, 2002/Tuff Huff
   Music, 2002/Zomba Songs, 2002
Performed by Avant on the album *Ecstasy* (MCA, 2002).

Mama's Baby Daddy's Maybe, see **Mama's Baby Poppa's Maybe.**

Mama's Baby Poppa's Maybe, also known as **Mama's Baby Daddy's
   Maybe**
Words and music by Jerry Williams and Gary Bonds
Jerry Williams Music, 1970/Sweet River Music, 1970
Covered by Green Eyez on the album *Me Against the World* (Bigg
   Mony Records, 2002) . Originally performed by Swamp Dogg on the
   album *Total Destruction to Your Mind* (Canyon, 1970).

Maria (Shut up and Kiss Me)
Words and music by Robert Thomas
Bidnis, 2002/EMI-Blackwood Music, 2002
Performed by Willie Nelson on the album *The Great Divide* (Lost
   Highway, 2002).

May It Be
Words by Roma Ryan, music by Enya (pseudonym for Eithne Ni
   Bhraonain) and Nicky Ryan
EMI-Blackwood Music, 2000
Performed by Enya in the movie and on the soundtrack album *The Lord
   of the Rings: The Fellowship of the Ring* (Reprise, 2001). Nominated
   for a Grammy Award, Best Song Written for a Motion Picture/
   Television, 2002.

Mendocino County Line
Words and music by Bernard Taupin and Matthew Serletic
Little Mole Music, 2002/Melusic Music, 2002
Performed by Willie Nelson featuring Lee Ann Womack on the album

The Great Divide (Lost Highway, 2002). Won a Grammy Award for Best Country Collaboration With Vocals, 2002. Nominated for a Grammy Award, Best Country Song, 2002.

Mentiroso
Words and music by Jose Garcia and Enrique Iglesias
EMI-April Music, 2002/Enrique Iglesias Music, 2002/Hey Chubby Music, 2002
Performed by Enrique Iglesias on the album *Quizas* (Universal Latino, 2002).

The Middle
Words and music by James Adkins, Richard Burch, Zachary Lind, and Thomas Linton
Dreamworks Songs, 2001/Turkey On Rye Music, 2001
Performed by Jimmy Eat World on the album *Bleed American* (DreamWorks, 2001).

Mine All Mine
Words and music by Kristyn Osborn and Hollie Poole
Lone Talisman Music, 2002/Without Anna Music, 2002
Performed by SHeDAISY on the soundtrack album *Sweet Home Alabama* (Hollywood, 2002). Also included on SHeDAISY's album *Knock on the Sky* (Hollywood, 2002).

Modern Day Bonnie and Clyde, also known as **Long Way to Richmond**
Words and music by James Aldridge and James Leblanc
EMI-April Music, 2000/House of Fame, 2000/Waltz Time Music, 2000
Performed by Travis Tritt on the album *Down the Road I Go* (Columbia, 2000).

A Moment Like This
Words and music by Jorgen Elofsson and John Reid
Careers-BMG Music Publishing, 2002/Sony ATV Songs LLC, 2002
Performed by Kelly Clarkson on the album *American Idol: Greatest Moments* (RCA, 2002).

More Than a Woman
Words and music by Stephen Garrett and Timbaland (pseudonym for Timothy Mosley)
Black Fountain Music, 2001/Herbilicious Music, 2001/Virginia Beach Music, 2001
Performed by Aaliyah on the album *I Care 4 U* (Blackground, 2002). Originally performed by Aaliyah on the album *Aaliyah* (Blackground, 2001). Nominated for a Grammy Award, Best Female R&B Vocal Performance, 2002.

More Than a Woman
Words and music by Edward Ferrell, Clifton Lighty, Darren Lighty, Bale'wa Muhammad, and Calvin Richardson
Eddie F. Music, Closter, 2001/I Want My Daddies Records, 2001/Sharay's Music, 2001/WB Music, 2001/Universal-Polygram International Tunes, 2001/Jahque Joints, 2001/Southern Boy Publishing, 2001
Performed by Angie Stone featuring Joe on the album *Mahogany Soul* (J, 2001). Nominated for a Grammy Award, Best R&B Performance by a Duo or Group With Vocal, 2002.

Most High
Words and music by Jerzee Monet (pseudonym for Tanisha Cary) and Tyrice Jones
EMI-Blackwood Music, 2002/Ground Control Music, 2002/N Key Music, 2002
Performed by Jerzee Monet on the album*Love & War* (DreamWorks, 2002).

Move Bitch
Words and music by Ludacris (pseudonym for Christopher Bridges), Mystikal (pseudonym for Michael Tyler), Craig Lawson, and Bobbi Sandimanie
Block off Broad Publishing, 2001/EMI-April Music, 2001/Ludacris Music Publishing, 2001/Zomba Enterprises, 2001
Performed by Ludacris featuring Mystikal and I-20 on the album *Word of Mouf* (Def Jam South, 2001).

Move It Like This
Words and music by Patrick Carey, Jeffrey Chea, Anthony Flowers, Colyn Grant, Steve Greenberg, Samuel Hollander, Brooke Morrow, Marvin Prosper, David Schommer, and Herschel Small
Deston Songs, 2002/Dreamworks Songs, 2002/Pop Rox Music, 2002/Cagey Music Publishing, 2002/Desmone Music, 2002/EMI-Blackwood Music, 2002/Godchildren Music, 2002/Riddum Music, 2002
Performed by Baha Men on the album *Greatest Movie Hits* (S-Curve, 2002).

MVP
Words and music by Jasper Cameron and Aliaune Thiam
139 7 Lenox Entertainment, 2002
Performed by Corey featuring Shaquille O'Neal on the album *I'm Just Corey* (Motown, 2002).

My Culture
Words and music by Duncan Bridgeman, Nigel Butler, James Catto, Maxwell Fraser, and Robert Williams

WB Music, 2001/BMG Music Publishing Ltd., 2001/Warner/Chappell
Music Ltd. (PRS), 2001/Bucks Music Ltd., 2001
Performed by 1 Giant Leap featuring Robbie Williams and Maxi Jazz
on the album *1 Giant Leap* (Palm Pictures, 2002). Nominated for a
Grammy Award, Best Short Form Music Video, 2002.

My Friends Over You

Words and music by Chad Gilbert, Cyrus Bolooki, Ian Grushka, Jordan
Pundik, and Stephen Klein
Blanco Meow Music, 2002/Universal Tunes, 2002
Performed by New Found Glory on the album *Sticks and Stones* (MCA,
2002).

My Heart Is Lost to You

Words and music by Brett Beavers and Connie Harrington
Sony ATV Tree Publishing, 2001/EMI-April Music, 2001
Performed by Brooks & Dunn on the album *Steers & Stripes* (Arista,
2001).

My List

Words and music by Rand Bishop and Tim James
Songwriters Paddock Music, 2001/Weightless Cargo Music, 2001/Song
Paddock Music, 2001
Performed by Toby Keith on the album *Unleashed* (DreamWorks,
2002).

My Neck My Back (Lick It), also known as Lick My Neck

Words by Khia Chambers, words and music by Edward Meriwether,
music by Michael Williams
R and Bling Music, 2001
Performed by Khia on the album *Thug Misses* (Artemis, 2002).

My Plague

Words and music by Michael Crahan, Christopher Fehn, Stephane
Gervais, Paul Gray, Craig Jones, Nathan Jordison, James Root, Corey
Taylor, and Sidney Wilson
EMI-April Music, 2001/Music That Music, 2001
Performed by Slipknot on the album *Iowa* (Roadrunner, 2001).
Nominated for a Grammy Award, Best Metal Performance, 2002.

My Sacrifice

Words and music by Scott Stapp and Mark Tremonti
Dwight Frye Music, 2001/Tremonti Stapp Music, 2001
Performed by Creed on the album *Weathered* (Wind-Up, 2001).
Nominated for a Grammy Award, Best Rock Performance by a Duo
or Group With Vocal, 2002.

My Town

Words and music by Jeffrey Steele (pseudonym for Jeff LeVasseur) and

George Nielsen
Gottahaveable Music, 2002/Singletrack Music, 2002/Songs of
  Windswept Pacific, 2002
Performed by Montgomery Gentry on the album *My Town* (Columbia,
  2002).

My Wild Beautiful Bird, see **Any Day Now**.

Mystery of Iniquity
Words and music by Lauryn Hill
Sony ATV Tunes LLC, 2002/Obverse Creation Music, 2002
Performed by Lauryn Hill on the album *MTV Unplugged No. 2.0*
  (Columbia, 2002). Nominated for a Grammy Award, Best Female Rap
  Solo Performance, 2002.

N

Na Na Be Like

Words and music by Foxy Brown (pseudonym for Inga Marchand),
 Kenya Miller, and Tamir Ruffin

North Avenue Music, 2001/Fame Brand Music, 2001

Performed by Foxy Brown on the album *Broken Silence* (Uptown/
 Universal, 2001). Originally appeared on the soundtrack album *Blue
 Streak* (Sony, 1999). Nominated for a Grammy Award, Best Female
 Rap Solo Performance, 2002.

The Need to Be Naked

Words and music by Johanna Cremers, James Harry, and William
 Steinberg

Jerk Awake Music, Los Angeles, 2002/EMI-Virgin Music, 2002/Marie
 Claire Music, 2002/Whorga Musica, 2002

Performed by Amber on the album *Naked* (Tommy Boy, 2002).

Never Again

Words and music by Chad Kroeger, music by Michael Kroeger, Ryan
 Peake, and Ryan Vikedal

Warner-Tamerlane Publishing, 2001

Performed by Nickelback on the album *Silver Side Up* (Roadrunner,
 2001).

Never Gonna Stop (The Red, Red Kroovy)

Words and music by Rob Zombie (pseudonym for Robert Cummings)
 and Scott Humphrey

Demonoid Deluxe Music, 2001/Gimme Back My Publishing, 2001/WB
 Music, 2001

Performed by Rob Zombie on the album *The Sinister Urge* (Universal,
 2001). Nominated for a Grammy Award, Best Metal Performance,
 2002.

A New Day Has Come

Words and music by Aldo Nova (pseudonym for Aldo Caporuscio) and
 Stephan Moccio

Deston Songs, 2002/Sony ATV Songs LLC, 2002
Performed by Celine Dion on the album *A New Day Has Come* (Epic,
2002).

The Night Inside Me
Words and music by Jackson Browne, music by Mark Goldenberg,
Mauricio Lewak, Kevin McCormick, and Jeffrey Young
Bacteria Music, 2002/Eye Cue Music, 2002/Glad Brad Music, 2002/
Swallow Turn Music, 2002/Bossy Pants Music, 2002/Songs of
Windswept Pacific, 2002
Performed by Jackson Browne on the album *The Naked Ride Home*
(Elektra, 2002).

No One Knows
Words and music by Josh Homme, Mark Lannegan, and Nick Oliveri
Board Stiff Music, 2002/Natural Light Music, 2002/Ripplestick Music,
2002
Performed by Queens of the Stone Age on the album *Songs for the Deaf*
(Interscope, 2002). Nominated for a Grammy Award, Best Hard Rock
Performance, 2002.

No Such Thing
Words and music by Douglas Cook and John Mayer
Specific Harm Music, 1999
Performed by John Mayer on the album *Room for Squares* (Aware,
2001). Song originally appeared on Mayer's album *Inside Wants Out*
(Aware, 1999).

Not a Day Goes By
Words and music by Maribeth Derry and Steven Diamond
American Broadcasting Music, 2001
Performed by Lonestar on the album *I'm Already There* (BNA, 2001).
Nominated for a Grammy Award, Best Country Performance by a
Duo/Group With Vocal, 2002.

Not Falling
Words and music by Chad Gray, Ryan Martinie, Matthew McDonough,
and Gregory Tribbett
Mudvayne Music, 2002/Zomba Enterprises, 2002
Performed by Mudvayne on the album *The End of All Things to Come*
(Epic, 2002).

Not Pretty Enough
Words and music by Kasey Chambers
Bughouse, 2001
Performed by Kasey Chambers on the album *Barricades & Brickwalls*
(Warner Bros., 2002).

Nothin'

Words and music by Noreaga (pseudonym for Victor Santiago) and
Pharrell Williams

EMI-Blackwood Music, 2002/Suite Twelve O Two Music, 2002/Waters
of Nazareth Publishing, 2002

Performed by N.O.R.E. on the album *God's Favorite* (Def Jam, 2002).

Nuclear

Words and music by Ryan Adams

Barland Music, 2002

Performed by Ryan Adams on the album *Demolition* (Lost Highway,
2002).

O

October Road
Words and music by James Taylor
Owl Rat Publishing, 2002
Performed by James Taylor on the album *October Road* (Columbia, 2002). Nominated for a Grammy Award, Best Male Pop Vocal Performance, 2002.

Off You
Words and music by Kim Deal
Period Music, 2002
Performed by the Breeders on the album *Title TK* (Elektra, 2002).

Oh Boy
Words and music by Cameron Giles, Justin Smith, and Norman Whitfield
FOB Music Publishing, 2002/Un Rivera Publishing, 2002/Warner-Tamerlane Publishing, 2002
Performed by Cam'ron featuring Juelz Santana on the album *Come Home With Me* (Roc-a-Fella, 2002). Nominated for a Grammy Award, Best Rap Performance by a Duo or Group, 2002.

Ol' Red
Words and music by James Bohon, Donald Goodman, and Mark Sherrill
Bull's Creek Publishing, 1990/Key Mark Music, 1990
Covered by Blake Shelton on the album *Blake Shelton* (Warner Bros., 2002). Originally performed by George Jones on the album *You Oughta Be Here With Me* (Columbia, 1990).

The One
Words and music by Karen Manno, music by Billy Lee (pseudonym for William Annaruma)
Lucky Girl Music, 2001/Migraine Music, 2001
Performed by Gary Allen on the album *Alright Guy* (MCA, 2001).

One Last Breath
Words and music by Scott Stapp and Mark Tremonti
Dwight Frye Music, 2002/Tremonti Stapp Music, 2002
Performed by Creed on the album *Weathered* (Wind-Up, 2002).

One Little Victory
Words by Neil Peart, music by Geddy Lee and Alex Lifeson
Warner-Tamerlane Publishing, 2002
Performed by Rush on the album *Vapor Trails* (Anthem/Atlantic, 2002).

One Mic
Words and music by Nas (pseudonym for Nasir Jones) and Charles
    Thompson
Ill Will Music, 2001/Zomba Enterprises, 2001/Ninth Street Tunnel
    Music, 2001/Sony ATV Songs LLC, 2001
Performed by Nas on the album *Stillmatic* (Ill Will, 2001). Nominated
    for a Grammy Award, Best Short Form Music Video, 2002.

One More Cup of Coffee
Words and music by Bob Dylan (pseudonym for Robert Zimmerman)
Sony ATV Tunes LLC, 1976
Covered by Robert Plant on the album *Dreamland* (Universal, 2002).
    Originally performed by Bob Dylan on the album *Desire* (Columbia,
    1976).

Only a Woman Like You
Words and music by Robert Lange, Shania Twain (pseudonym for
    Eileen Regina Lange), Max Martin (pseudonym for Martin
    Sandberg), and Rami (pseudonym for Rami Yacoub)
Zomba Enterprises, 2002/Loon Echo Music, 2002/Universal Songs of
    Polygram Intntl., 2002
Performed by Michael Bolton on the album *Only a Woman Like You*
    (Jive, 2002).

Oops (Oh My)
Words and music by Melissa Elliott, Tweet (pseudonym for Charlene
    Keys), and Timbaland (pseudonym for Timothy Mosley)
Fo Shawna Productions, 2002/Mass Confusion Productions, 2002/
    Virginia Beach Music, 2002/WB Music, 2002
Performed by Tweet on the album *Southern Hummingbird* (Goldmind/
    Elektra, 2002).

Opposites Attract (What They Like)
Words and music by Fat Joe (pseudonym for Joseph Cartagena), Jesse
    Farrow, Edward Hinson, Irv Gotti (pseudonym for Irving Lorenzo),
    and Remy Smith
DJ Irv Publishing, 2001/Ensign Music, 2001/Irving Music, 2001/Tiarra's
    Daddy Music, 2001/Dreaming Jewels Music, 2001/Songs of

Universal, 2001/Joseph Cartagena Music, 2001/Jelly's Jams LLC Music, 2001

Performed by Fat Joe featuring Remy on the album *Jealous Ones Still Envy (J.O.S.E.)* (Atlantic, 2001).

Ordinary Day

Words and music by Vanessa Carlton

Rosasharn Music, 2002/Songs of Universal, 2002

Performed by Vanessa Carlton on the album *Be Not Nobody* (Universal, 2002).

Original Sin

Words by Bernard Taupin, music by Elton John (pseudonym for Reginald Dwight)

Warner-Tamerlane Publishing, 2001/Wretched Music, 2001

Performed by Elton John on the album *Songs From the West Coast* (MCA, 2001). Nominated for a Grammy Award, Best Male Pop Vocal Performance, 2002.

Osama-Yo' Mama

Words and music by Ray Stevens (pseudonym for Harold Ray Ragsdale) and Cyrus W. Kalb, Jr

Ray Stevens Music, 2001

Performed by Ray Stevens on the album *Osama-Yo' Mama* (Curb, 2002).

The Other Side

Words and music by David Gray

Chrysalis Songs, 2002

Performed by David Gray on the album *New Day at Midnight* (RCA, 2002).

Out of My Heart

Words and music by Anthony Griffiths, Chris Griffiths, Stephen McNally, Christian Burns, and Mark Barry

Famous Music, 2002/Strongsongs Ltd., 2002

Performed by BBMak on the album *Into Your Head* (Hollywood, 2002).

Overprotected

Words and music by Max Martin (pseudonym for Martin Sandberg) and Rami (pseudonym for Rami Yacoub)

Zomba Enterprises, 2001

Performed by Britney Spears on the album *Britney* (Jive, 2001). Nominated for a Grammy Award, Best Female Pop Vocal Performance, 2002.

P

Paid My Dues
Words and music by LaMenga Ford, Gregory Lawson, Anastacia
 Newkirk, and Damon Reinagle
Annotation Music, 2001/Damon Sharpe Music, 2001/La Coriya's Songs,
 2001/Po Ho Productions, 2001/Universal Music Publishing, 2001/WB
 Music, 2001/Connotation Music, 2001/GQ Romeo Music, 2001
Performed by Anastacia on the album *Freak of Nature* (Epic/Daylight,
 2001).

Papa Don't Preach
Words and music by Brian Elliot
Elliot/Jacobsen Music Publishing, 1986
Covered by Kelly Osbourne on the album *The Osbourne Family Album*
 (Epic, 2002). Also included on Osbourne's album *Shut Up* (Epic,
 2002). Originally performed by Madonna on the album *True Blue*
 (Sire, 1986).

Party Hard
Words and music by Andrew Wilkes-Krier
Andrew WK Music, 2002
Performed by Andrew W.K. on the album *I Get Wet* (Island, 2002).

Party 'til You Puke
Words and music by Andrew Wilkes-Krier
Andrew WK Music, 2002
Performed by Andrew W.K. on the album *I Get Wet* (Island, 2002).

Pass the Courvoisier Pt. 2
Words and music by Charles Hugo, Busta Rhymes (pseudonym for
 Trevor Smith), Pharrell Williams, P. Diddy (pseudonym for Sean
 Combs), Jermaine Denny, Bernard Edwards, Kamaal Fareed, Bryan
 Higgins, James Jackson, Muhammad Jones, Dominick Lamb, Sandy
 Linzer, Denny Randell, Nile Rodgers, Malik Taylor, Mystikal
 (pseudonym for Michael Tyler), and Jamal Woolard
EMI-April Music, 2001/Bernard's Other Music, 2001/Denny Randell

Music, 2001/EMI-Blackwood Music, 2001/Ensign Music, 2001/
Featherbed Music Inc., 2001/Sony ATV Songs LLC, 2001/Teamsta
Entertainment Music, 2001/Tziah Music, 2001/Warner-Tamerlane
Publishing, 2001/Waters of Nazareth Publishing, 2001/Chase Chad
Music, 2001
Performed by Busta Rhymes featuring P. Diddy and Pharrell on the
album *Totally Hits 2002* (Warner Bros./BMG, 2002). Nominated for a
Grammy Award, Best Rap Performance by a Duo or Group, 2002.

Picture
Words and music by Sheryl Crow and Kid Rock (pseudonym for Robert
Ritchie)
Old Crow Music, 2001/Thirty Two Mile Music, 2001/Warner-Tamerlane
Publishing, 2001
Performed by Kid Rock featuring Allison Moorer. Released as a single
(Universal South, 2002). Originally performed by Kid Rock and
Sheryl Crow on the Kid Rock album *Cocky* (Lava, 2001).

Playing With Fire
Music by Kirk Whalum, Paul Brown, and Robert Vally
Whalumusic, 2000/Carnevalli Music, 2000/Songs of Universal, 2000/Yo
Cats Music, 2000
Performed by Kirk Whalum on the album *Unconditional* (Warner Bros.,
2000). Nominated for a Grammy Award, Best Pop Instrumental
Performance, 2002.

Po' Folks
Words and music by Kenneth Anthony, William Hughes, Joe Kent, Vito
Tisdale, and Mark Williams
Notting Dale Songs, London, England, 2002/Tarpo Music Publishing,
London, England, 2002/Nappy Roots Publishing, 2002
Performed by Nappy Roots featuring Anthony Hamilton on the album
Watermelon, Chicken and Gritz (Atlantic, 2002). Nominated for a
Grammy Award, Best Rap/Sung Collaboration, 2002.

Pocketbook
Words and music by Me'Shell Ndegeocello
Revolutionary Jazz Giant, 2002/Warner-Tamerlane Publishing, 2002
Performed by Me'Shell NdegeOcello with Redman and Tweet on the
album *Cookie: the Anthropological Mix Tape* (Maverick, 2002).

Por Ese Hombre
Words and music by Joaquin Galan and Lucia Glan
EMI-Blackwood Music, 1985
Covered by Brenda K. Starr featuring Tito Nieves and Victor Manuelle
on the album *Temptation* (Sony Discos, 2002). Originally performed
by Pimpinella on the album *Lucia y Joaquin* (Sony, 1985).

Portrait
Words and music by Noah Bernardo, Marcos Curiel, Mark Daniels, and Paul Sandoval
Famous Music, 2001/Souljah Music, 2001
Performed by P.O.D. on the album *Satellite* (Atlantic, 2001). Nominated for a Grammy Award, Best Metal Performance, 2002.

Prayer
Words and music by Dan Donegan, David Draiman, Steve Kmak, and Michael Wengren
Mother Culture Publishing, 2000/WB Music, 2000
Performed by Disturbed on the album *Believe* (Warner Bros., 2002).

Precious Illusions
Words and music by Alanis Morissette
1974 Music, 2002/Universal-MCA Music Publishing, 2002
Performed by Alanis Morissette on the album *Under Rug Swept* (Maverick, 2002). Also appears on Morissette's album *Feast on Scraps* (Maverick, 2002).

Put It on Paper
Words and music by Timothy Lee, Herbert Middleton, Lula Ann Nesby, Jamal Orr, and Michael Orr
Labor Force Publishing, 2002/Mr. Perry's Music Publishing, 2002/ Bachus Music, 2002/Big Herb's Music, 2002/Embassy Music, 2002/ Songs of Lastrada, 2002/Sony ATV Songs LLC, 2002
Performed by Ann Nesby featuring Al Green on the album *Put It on Paper* (Universal, 2002). Nominated for a Grammy Award, Best Traditional R&B Vocal Performance, 2002.

Put Yo Sets Up
Words and music by Juvenile (pseudonym for Terius Gray), Brandy Martin, and James Pierre
Z Bo and Happy Publishing, 2002
Performed by Redd Eyezz featuring Juvenile and Slanted Eyezz on the album *We Gotta Eat* (Rufflife, 2002).

R

Rainfall
Words by Robert Schneider, music by Kilarie Sidney
Elephant 6 Publishing, 2002
Performed by the Apples in Stereo on the album *Velocity of Sound* (spinART, 2002).

Rainy Dayz
Words by Ja Rule (pseudonym for Jeffrey Atkins), music by Irv Gotti (pseudonym for Irving Lorenzo)
DJ Irv Publishing, 2002/Ensign Music, 2002/Slavery Music, 2002/Songs of Universal, 2002
Performed by Mary J. Blige featuring Ja Rule on the album *No More Drama* (MCA, 2002). Also appears on her album *Dance for Me* (MCA, 2002).

React
Words and music by Reggie Noble, Erick Sermon, and J. Smith
Notting Dale Songs, London, England, 2002
Performed by Erick Sermon featuring Redman on the album *React* (J, 2002).

The Red
Words and music by Peter Loeffler
Loeffler Music, 2002/WB Music, 2002
Performed by Chevelle on the album *Wonder What's Next* (Epic, 2002).

Red Ragtop
Words and music by Jason White
Sony/ATV Acuff Rose Music, 2001
Covered by Tim McGraw & the Dancehall Doctors on the album *Tim McGraw & the Dancehall Doctors* (Curb, 2002). Originially performed by Jason White on the album *Shades of Gray* (Hanging Vines, 2001).

Right Here, Right Now
Words and music by Ling Gray, Erik De Koning, Paul Oakenfold,
    Stephen Osborne, and Ice Cube (pseudonym for O'Shea Jackson)
EMI-Virgin Music, 2002/Songs of Windswept Pacific, 2002
Performed by Ice Cube and Paul Oakenfold on the soundtrack album
    Blade II (Virgin, 2002).

The Rising
Words and music by Bruce Springsteen
Bruce Springsteen Publishing, 2002
Performed by Bruce Springsteen on the album *The Rising* (Columbia,
    2002). Won Grammy Awards. Nominated for a Grammy Award,
    Song of the Year, 2002.

Rocksteady
Words and music by Remy Shand
Mortay Music Ltd., 2002
Performed by Remy Shand on the album *The Way I Feel* (Motown,
    2002). Nominated for a Grammy Award, Best Traditional R&B Vocal
    Performance, 2002.

Roll on John
Traditional
Performed by Bob Dylan on the album *There Is No Eye: Music for
    Photographs* (Smithsonian Folkways, 2001).

Roll the Stone Away
Words and music by Jeff Hanna and Marcus Hummon
Careers-BMG Music Publishing, 2002/Mother Tracy Music, 2002/Our
    Trinity Music, 2002/Warner-Tamerlane Publishing, 2002
Performed by Nitty Gritty Dirt Band on the album *Will the Circle Be
    Unbroken, Vol. III* (Capitol, 2002). Nominated for a Grammy Award,
    Best Country Performance by a Duo/Group With Vocal, 2002.

Rollout (My Business)
Words and music by Ludacris (pseudonym for Christopher Bridges) and
    Timbaland (pseudonym for Timothy Mosley)
Ludacris Music Publishing, 2001/Virginia Beach Music, 2001/WB
    Music, 2001
Performed by Ludacris on the album *Word of Mouf* (Def Jam South,
    2001). Nominated for a Grammy Award, Best Male Rap Solo
    Performance, 2002.

Round and Round
Words and music by Hi-Tek (pseudonym for Tony Cottrell) and
    Shannon Showes
Scribble Ink Publishing, 2001/513 Music, 2001/DJ Hi Tek Music
    Publishing, 2001/Shannon River Music, 2001/Songs of Windswept

Pacific, 2001

Performed by Hi-Tek featuring Jonell and Method Man on the album *Hi-Teknology* (Priority, 2001).

Run

Words and music by Tony Lane and Ralph Smith

Almo Music, 2001/Famous Music, 2001

Performed by George Strait on the album *The Road Less Traveled* (MCA, 2001).

Running Away

Words and music by Daniel Estrin, Chris Hesse, Markku Lappalainen, and Douglas Robb

Spread Your Cheeks, 2001/WB Music, 2001

Performed by Hoobastank on the album *Hoobastank* (Universal, 2001).

S

Sacred and Profane
Words and music by Billy Corgan
Faust's Haus Music, 2000
Covered by Berlin on the album *Voyeur* (Artist Direct, 2002). Originally
  performed by Smashing Pumpkins on the album *Machina/The
  Machines of God* (Virgin, 2000).

Sally Goodin
Traditional
Performed by the Chieftains featuring Earl Scruggs on the album *Down
  the Old Plank Road: The Nashville Sessions* (RCA, 2002). Nominated
  for a Grammy Award, Best Country Instrumental Performance, 2002.

Satellite
Words and music by Noah Bernardo, Marcos Curiel, Mark Daniels, and
  Paul Sandoval
Famous Music, 2001/Souljah Music, 2001
Performed by P.O.D. on the album *Satellite* (Atlantic, 2001).

Satisfaction
Words and music by Eve (pseudonym for Eve Jeffers), Michael
  Elizondo, and Dr. Dre (pseudonym for Andre Young)
Ain't Nothing but Funkin' Music, 2002/Blondie Rockwell Music, 2002/
  Blotter Music, 2002/Elvis Mambo Music, 2002/Music of Windswept,
  2002/WB Music, 2002
Performed by Eve on the album *Eve-Olution* (Interscope, 2002).
  Nominated for a Grammy Award, Best Female Rap Solo
  Performance, 2002.

Saturday (Oooh! Ooooh!)
Words and music by Ludacris (pseudonym for Christopher Bridges) and
  Rico Wade, music by Sleepy Brown and Ramon Murray
EMI-April Music, 2001/Ludacris Music Publishing, 2001/Organized
  Noize Music, 2001

Performed by Ludacris featuring Sleepy Brown on the album *Word of Mouf* (Def Jam South, 2001).

Say You'll Be Mine
Words and music by Gary Louris and Mark Olson
Absinthe Music, 2002/Sunny Vista Music, 2002
Performed by Mark Olson & the Creekdippers on the album *December's Child* (Dualtone, 2002).

Sco-Mule
Music by Warren Haynes
Buzzard Rock Music, 2001
Performed by Gov't Mule on the album *The Deep End, Vol. 2* (ATO, 2002). Originally appeared on Gov't Mule's album *The Deep End, Vol. 1* (ATO, 2001). Nominated for a Grammy Award, Best Rock Instrumental Performance, 2002.

Scream A.K.A. Itchin'
Words and music by Melissa Elliott and Timbaland (pseudonym for Timothy Mosley)
Mass Confusion Productions, 2001/Virginia Beach Music, 2001/WB Music, 2001
Performed by Missy Elliott on the soundtrack album *The Transporter* (Elektra, 2002). Originally appeared on Elliot's album *Miss E. . . So Addictive* (Goldmind/Elektra, 2001). Won a Grammy Award for Best Female Rap Solo Performance, 2002.

Selah
Words and music by Lauryn Hill
Obverse Creation Music, 2002/Sony ATV Tunes LLC, 2002
Performed by Lauryn Hill on the soundtrack album *Divine Secrets of the Ya-Ya Sisterhood* (DMZ/Columbia, 2002).

7 Days
Words and music by Craig David, Darren Hill, and Mark Hill
Music of Windswept, 2001/WB Music, 2001
Performed by Craig David on the album *Born to Do It* (Atlantic, 2001). Nominated for a Grammy Award, Best Male Pop Vocal Performance, 2002.

She Hates Me
Words and music by Wesley Scantlin and James Allen
Jordan Rocks Music, 2001/Stereo Supersonic Music, 2001/WB Music, 2001
Performed by Puddle of Mudd on the album *Come Clean* (Flawless, 2001).

She Loves Me Not
Words and music by David Buckner, Tobin Esperance, Jerry Horton,

and Jacoby Shaddix
Dreamworks Songs, 2000/Viva La Cucaracha Music, 2000
Performed by Papa Roach on the album *lovehatetragedy* (DreamWorks, 2002).

She Was
Words and music by Neal Coty and James Melton
Melanie Howard Music, Nashville, 2001/Murrah Music, 2001
Performed by Mark Chesnutt on the album *Mark Chesnutt* (Columbia, 2002).

She'll Leave You With a Smile
Words and music by Odie Blackmon and Jay Knowles
Big Yellow Dog Music, 2001/Sony ATV Tree Publishing, 2001/Cal IV
  Entertainment, 2001/Larga Vista Music, 2001
Performed by George Strait on the album *The Road Less Traveled*
  (MCA, 2001).

Shine
Words and music by Meredith Brooks, David Darling, and Shelly
  Peiken
EMI-Blackwood Music, 2002/Kissing Booth Music, 2002/Peermusic III,
  2002/Shellayla Songs, 2002
Performed by Meredith Brooks on the album *Bad Bad One* (Gold
  Circle, 2002).

Shine
Words and music by David Lowery and John Hickman
Bad Alter Boy Music, 2002/Bicycle Spanaird Music, 2002/Funzalo
  Music, 2002
Performed by Cracker on the album *Shine* (Back Porch, 2002).

Shut Up
Words and music by Kelly Osbourne, Mike Benigno, Kara Dioguardi,
  Chris Goercke, Marc Russell, Ric Wake, and Thomas Yezzi
K Stuff Publishing, 2002/Marc Russel Songs, 2002/Yezzimuzic, 2002/
  Milkbean Music, 2002/444 Days, 2002
Performed by Kelly Osbourne on the album *Shut Up* (Epic, 2002).

Si Tu Te Vas
Words and music by Escolar Gomez, Cheryl Rubin, and Joshua Rubin
E Two Music, 2002/Groobin Music, 2002/Hear Yie Music, 2002/
  Universal Music Publishing, 2002
Performed by Paulina Rubio on the album *Border Girl* (Universal,
  2002).

Silver Lining
Words and music by David Gray
Chrysalis Music, 1999

Covered by Bonnie Raitt on the album *Silver Lining* (Capitol, 2001).
  Originally performed by David Gray on the album *White Ladder*
  (IHT, 1999).

Six Days
Words and music by Josh Davis, Brian Farrell, and Denis Olivieri
Universal Music Publishing, 2002
Performed by DJ Shadow on the album *The Private Press* (MCA,
  2002).

Sk8er Boi
Words and music by Scott Spock (pseudonym for David Alspach),
  Graham Edwards, Lauren Christy (pseudonym for Lauren Fownes),
  and Avril Lavigne
Almo Music, 2002/Ferry Hill Songs, 2002/WB Music, 2002/Mr. Spock
  Music, 2002/Rainbow Fish Publishing, 2002/Warner-Tamerlane
  Publishing, 2002
Performed by Avril Lavigne on the album *Let Go* (Arista, 2002).
  Nominated for a Grammy Award, Best Female Rock Vocal
  Performance, 2002.

Slow Burn
Words and music by David Bowie (pseudonym for David Jones)
Nipple Music, 2002
Performed by David Bowie on the album *Heathen* (ISO/Columbia,
  2002). Nominated for a Grammy Award, Best Male Rock Vocal
  Performance, 2002.

Smoothie Song
Music by Chris Thile
Southern Melody Publishing, 2002
Performed by Nickel Creek on the album *This Side* (Sugar Hill, 2002).
  Nominated for a Grammy Award, Best Country Instrumental
  Performance, 2002.

Soak up the Sun
Words and music by Sheryl Crow and Jeff Trott
Old Crow Music, 2002/Cyrillic Soup, 2002
Performed by Sheryl Crow on the album *c'mon, c'mon* (A&M, 2002).
  Nominated for a Grammy Award, Best Female Pop Vocal
  Performance, 2002.

Some Days You Gotta Dance
Words and music by Troy Johnson and Marshall Morgan
Beavers Brand Music, 1997/Song Auction Music, 1997/Sony ATV
  Tunes LLC, 1997
Covered by Nashville Girls of Country on the album *A Tribute to Dixie*

Chicks (Big Eye, 2002). Originally performed by Ranch on the album *Ranch* (Capital, 1997).

Somebody Let the Devil Out
Words and music by Popa Chubby (pseudonym for Theodore Horowitz)
Dutchdaddy Music, 2002
Performed by Popa Chubby on the album *The Good, the Bad and the Chubby* (Blind Pig, 2002.)

Somebody Like You
Words and music by John Shanks and Keith Urban
Coburn Music, 2002/Dylan Jackson Music, 2002/WB Music, 2002
Performed by Keith Urban on the album *Golden Road* (Capitol, 2002).

Someday
Words and music by Julian Casablancas
The Strokes Band Music, 2001
Performed by the Strokes on the album *Is This It?* (RCA, 2001).

Someone to Love You
Words and music by Mark Rooney
Cori Tiffani Publishing, 2002/Sony ATV Songs LLC, 2002
Performed by Ruff Endz on the soundtrack album *Down to Earth* (Sony, 2001). Also appears on Ruff Endz' album *Someone to Love You* (Epic, 2002).

Something
Words and music by Peter Lutz and David Vervoort
EMI-Blackwood Music, 2001
Performed by Lasgo on the album *Some Things* (EMI, 2001).

Something Worth Leaving Behind
Words and music by Brett Beavers and Tom Douglas
Sony ATV Tree Publishing, 2002
Performed by Lee Ann Womack on the album*Something Worth Leaving Behind* (MCA, 2002). Nominated for a Grammy Award, Best Female Country Vocal Performance, 2002.

Somewhere in the Middle
Words and music by John Richards, music by Scott Alexander, Rodney Cravens, Peter Maloney, Gregg Wattenberg, and James Wood
600 Foot Hedgehog Music, 2002/EMI-April Music, 2002/T H I O, 2002
Performed by Dishwalla on the album *Opaline* (Immergent, 2002).

Song Cry
Words by Jay-Z (pseudonym for Shawn Carter), music by Douglas Gibbs and Ralph Johnson
Chitty Chitty Music, 2001/Extraslick Music, 2001/EMI-Blackwood Music, 2001/Lil Lu Lu Publishing, 2001

Performed by Jay-Z on the album *The Blueprint* (Uptown/Universal, 2001). Also appears on the Jay-Z album *Unplugged* (Def Jam, 2001). Nominated for a Grammy Award, Best Male Rap Solo Performance, 2002.

Song for the Lonely
Words and music by Paul Barry, Steve Torch, and Mark Taylor
Rive Droite Music, 2001/Metrophonic Music, 2001
Performed by Cher on the album *Living Proof* (Warner Bros., 2002).

The Sound of Goodbye
Words and music by Adrian Broekhuyse, Armin Van Buuren, and E. Moore
Universal Polygram International Pub., 2001/Razmataz Songs, 2001
Performed by Perpetuous Dreamer on the album *The Sound of Goodbye* (Armind, 2001).

South Wind of Summer
Words and music by Earle Ely, Jimmie Dale Gilmore, and George Hancock
Irving Music, 1998/Jade EG Music, 1998/Tornado Temple Music, 1998/ Two Bagger Music, 1998/Two Roads Music, 1998
Performed by the Flatlanders on the album *Now Again* (New West, 2002). Originally appeared on the soundtrack album *The Horse Whisperer* (MCA, 1998).

Squeeze Me In
Words and music by Delbert McClinton and Gary Nicholson
Cross Keys Publishing, 1995/Four Sons Music, 1995/Nasty Cat Music, 1995
Covered by Garth Brooks featuring Trisha Yearwood on the album *Scarecrow* (Capitol, 2001). Originally performed by Lee Roy Parnell on the album *We All Get Lucky Sometimes* (Career, 1995). Nominated for a Grammy Award, Best Country Collaboration With Vocals, 2002.

Stairway to Heaven
Words and music by James Page and Robert Plant
Superhype Publishing, 1972
Covered by Dolly Parton on the album *Halos & Horns* (Sugar Hill, 2002). Originally performed by Led Zeppelin on the album *Led Zeppelin IV* (Atlantic, 1971).

Standing Still
Words and music by Jewel Kilcher and Richard Nowels
EMI-April Music, 2001/Future Furniture, 2001/WB Music, 2001/Wiggly Tooth Music, 2001
Performed by Jewel on the album *This Way* (Atlantic, 2001).

Starry Eyed Surprise
Words and music by Seth Binzer, Mike Maddox, Fred Neil, and Paul
  Oakenfold
Songs of Windswept Pacific, 2002/Third Palm Music, 2002
Performed by Paul Oakenfold featuring Shifty Shellshock on the album
  Bunkka (Maverick, 2002).

Starry Night
Music by Joe Satriani
Strange Beautiful Music, 2002
Performed by Joe Satriani on the album *Strange Beautiful Music* (Epic,
  2002). Nominated for a Grammy Award, Best Rock Instrumental
  Performance, 2002.

Stepchild
Words and music by Bob Dylan (pseudonym for Robert Zimmerman)
Special Rider Music, 1978
Performed by Solomon Burke on the album *Don't Give up on Me* (Fat
  Possum, 2002).

Steve McQueen
Words and music by Sheryl Crow and John Shanks
Old Crow Music, 2002/Warner-Tamerlane Publishing, 2002/Dylan
  Jackson Music, 2002/WB Music, 2002
Performed by Sheryl Crow on the album *c'mon, c'mon* (A&M, 2002).
  Won a Grammy Award for Best Female Rock Vocal Performance,
  2002.

Still Fly
Words and music by Byron Thomas and Bryan Williams
Money Mack Music, 2002
Performed by Big Tymers on the soundtrack album *XXX* (Universal,
  2002). Also appears on their album *Hood Rich* (Cash Money, 2002).
  Nominated for a Grammy Award, Best Rap Performance by a Duo or
  Group, 2002.

Still Not Over You
Words and music by Natasha Belton, Tokiko George, Andre Harris,
  Jolyon Skinner, and Latoya Watson
Dirty Dre Music, 2001/Jat Cat Music Publishing, 2001/Universal Music
  Publishing, 2001
Performed by Exhale on the album *Exhale* (Town Sound, 2001).

Stillness of Heart
Words and music by Leonard Kravitz and Craig Ross
Miss Bessie Music, 2001/Wigged Music, 2001
Performed by Lenny Kravitz on the album *Lenny* (Virgin, 2001).

Stingy
Words and music by Johnta Austin, Bryan Cox, and Jason Perry
Chrysalis Music, 2002/Naked Under My Clothes Music, 2002/Babyboys
    Little Pub Co, 2002/Jasons Lyrics, 2002/Noontime South, 2002/WB
    Music, 2002
Performed by Ginuwine on the soundtrack album *Barbershop* (Sony,
    2002).

Stole
Words and music by Dane DeViller, Syed Hosein, and Stephen Kipner
Big Caboose Music, 2002/BMG Songs, 2002/Little Engine
    Entertainment, 2002/Sonic Grafitti, 2002
Performed by Kelly Rowland on the album *Simply Deep* (Sony, 2002).

The Streets
Words and music by Snoop Dogg (pseudonym for Calvin Broadus), WC
    (pseudonym for William Calhoun), Nate Dogg (pseudonym for
    Nathaniel Hale), and Scott Storch
Base Pipe Music, 2002/TVT Music, 2002/Nate Dogg Music, 2002/My
    Own Chit Publishing, 2002
WC featuring Snoop Dogg and Nate Dogg on the album *Ghetto
    Heisman* (Def Jam, 2002).

Strong Enough to Be Your Man
Words and music by Travis Tritt
Post Oak Publishing, 2002
Performed by Travis Tritt on the album *Strong Enough* (Columbia,
    2002).

Suerte (Whenever, Wherever)
Words and music by Shakira Mebarak, music by Timothy Mitchell
FIPP International, 2001/Sony/ATV Latin Music Publishing, 2001
Performed by Shakira on the album *Laundry Service* (Sony, 2001).

Sugarhigh
Words and music by Jade Anderson and Francis White
WB Music, 2002
Performed by Jade Anderson on the album *Dive Deeper* (Sony, 2002).

Supersonic
Words and music by Greg Graffin and Brett Gurewitz
EMI-Blackwood Music, 2002/Polypterus Music, 2002/Sick Muse Songs,
    2002
Performed by Bad Religion on the album *The Process of Belief*
    (Epitaph, 2002).

Superstylin'
Words and music by Andy Cato (pseudonym for Andrew Cocup), Tom
    Findlay, Michael Davies, Jonathan White, and Keeling Lee

Warner/Chappell Music Ltd. (PRS), 2001/WB Music, 2001/Universal Polygram International Pub., 2001/Copyright Control Music, 2001/ Zomba Enterprises, 2001

Performed by Groove Armada on the album *goodbye country (hello nightclub)* (Jive, 2001). Nominated for a Grammy Award, Best Dance Recording, 2002.

Sweetness

Words and music by James Adkins, Richard Burch, Zachary Lind, and Thomas Linton

Dreamworks Songs, 2001/Turkey On Rye Music, 2001

Performed by Jimmy Eat World on the album *Bleed American* (DreamWorks, 2001).

T

Take Me As I Am
Words and music by Emerson Hart and Daniel Lavery
Big Ass Pete, 2002/EMI-April Music, 2002/Skizzneck Music, 2002
Performed by Tonic on the album *Head on Straight* (Universal, 2002).
Nominated for a Grammy Award, Best Rock Performance by a Duo
or Group With Vocal, 2002.

Take a Message
Words and music by Remy Shand
Mortay Music Ltd., 2002
Performed by Remy Shand on the album *The Way I Feel* (Motown,
2002). Nominated for Grammy Awards, Best Male R&B Vocal
Performance, 2002, and Best R&B Song, 2002.

Take My Hand (remix)
Words and music by Dido (pseudonym for Dido Armstrong) and
Richard Dekkard
WB Music, 2001
Performed by Dido on the album *No Angel* (Arista, 2001).

Ten Rounds With Jose Cuervo
Words and music by Casey Beathard, Marla Cannon, and Michael
Heeney
Sony/ATV Acuff Rose Music, 2001/Big Purple Dog, 2001/Sony ATV
Tunes LLC, 2001
Performed by Tracy Byrd on the album *Ten Rounds* (RCA, 2001).

That's Just Jessie
Words and music by Kevin Denney, Patrick Matthews, and Kerry
Phillips
Maleahk Music, 2002/March Family Music, 2002/EMI-April Music,
2002/Sufferin Succotash Songs, 2002/Zomba Enterprises, 2002
Performed by Kevin Denney on the album *Kevin Denney* (Lyric Street,
2002).

That's When I Love You
Words and music by Julie Vassar and Phil Vassar
EMI-April Music, 2000/Phil Vassar Music, 2000
Performed by Phil Vassar on the album *Totally Country* (Sony, 2002).
   Song previously appeared on Vassar's album *Phil Vassar* (Arista,
   2000).

There Goes the Fear
Words and music by Jamie Goodwin, Andrew Williams, and Jeremy
   Williams
EMI-April Music, 2002
Performed by Doves on the album *The Last Broadcast* (Capitol, 2002).

These Days
Words and music by Steve Robson, Jeffrey Steele, and Danny Wells
Gottahaveable Music, 2002/Irving Music, 2002/Songs of Teracel, 2002/
   Songs of Windswept Pacific, 2002/Sony ATV Tree Publishing, 2002/
   Rondo Music London (PRS), 2002
Performed by Rascal Flatts on the album *Melt* (Lyric Street, 2002).

They-Say Vision
Words and music by Martin McKinney and Santi White
She Writes Her Own Music, 2001
Performed by Res on the album *How I Do* (MCA, 2001).

Things That Scare Me
Words and music by Neko Case and Tom Ray
Nedotykomka, 2001/Ray Farm Music, 2001
Performed by Neko Case on the album *Blacklisted* (Bloodshot, 2002).

This Train Don't Stop There Anymore
Words by Bernard Taupin, music by Elton John (pseudonym for
   Reginald Dwight)
Warner-Tamerlane Publishing, 2001/Wretched Music, 2001
Performed by Elton John on the album *Songs From the West Coast*
   (MCA, 2001).

Thoughtless
Words and music by Fieldy (pseudonym for Reginald Arvizu), Jonathan
   Davis, James Shaffer, David Silveria, and Brian Welch
Evileria Music, 2002/Fieldysnuttz Music, 2002/Gintoe Music, 2002/
   Musik Munk Publishing, 2002/Stratosphericyoness Music, 2002/
   Zomba Songs, 2002
Performed by Korn on the album *Untouchables* (Epic, 2002).

A Thousand Miles
Words and music by Vanessa Carlton
Rosasharn Music, 2002/Songs of Universal, 2002
Performed by Vanessa Carlton on the album *Be Not Nobody* (A&M,

2002). Nominated for Grammy Awards, Record of the Year, 2002, and Song of the Year, 2002.

'03 Bonnie & Clyde

Words and music by Jay-Z (pseudonym for Shawn Carter), Darryl Harper, Prince (pseudonym for Prince Nelson), Ricky Rouse, Tupac Shakur, K. West, and Tyrone Wrice

WB Music, 2002/Songs of Universal, 2002/Suge Publishing, 2002/ Universal Music Publishing, 2002

Performed by Jay-Z featuring Beyonce Knowles on the album *The Blueprint2: The Gift & the Curse* (Def Jam, 2002).

Three Days

Words and music by Radney Foster and Pat Green

EMI-Blackwood Music, 2001/Greenhorse Music, 2001/Spunkersongs, 2001/Universal Polygram International Pub., 2001

Performed by Pat Green on the album *Three Days* (Republic/Universal, 2002). Nominated for Grammy Awards, Best Country Song, 2002, and Best Male Country Vocal Performance, 2002.

To Where You Are

Words and music by Richard Marx and Linda Thompson

Brandon Brody Music, 2001/Warner-Tamerlane Publishing, 2001/Chi-Boy Music, 2001

Performed by Josh Groban on the album *Josh Groban in Concert* (Warner Bros., 2002). Originally performed by Groban on the album *Josh Groban* (Warner Bros., 2001).

Tomorrow

Words and music by Mitchell Scherr

EMI-April Music, 2002/Matzoh Ball Music, 2002

Performed by SR-71 on the album *Tomorrow* (RCA, 2002).

Tonight I Wanna Be Your Man

Words and music by Melvern Rutherford and Thomas Verges

Memphisto Music, 2002/Universal-MCA Music Publishing, 2002/Songs of Universal, 2002

Performed by Andy Griggs on the album *Freedom* (RCA, 2002).

Toxicity

Words and music by Serj Tankian, music by Daron Malakian and Shavarsh Odadjian

Ddevil Music, 2001/Sony Tunes, 2001

Performed by System of a Down on the album *Toxicity (American/ Columbia, 2001). Also appears on the album The Pledge of Allegiance Tour: Live Concert Recording* (Columbia, 2002).

Trade It All

Words and music by Ernesto Shaw, Brandon Casey, Brian Casey, and

Fabolous (pseudonym for John Jackson), music by Kenneth Ifill
Air Control Music, 2001/EMI-April Music, 2001/J Brasco, 2001/Them
    Damn Twins Music, 2001/Duro Music, 2001/EMI-Blackwood Music,
    2001/Mr. Manatti Music, 2001
Performed by Fabolous featuring P. Diddy and Jagged Edge on the
    album *Ghetto Fabolous* (Elektra, 2002).

Two Months Off
Words and music by Karl Hyde and Richard Smith
Warner-Tamerlane Publishing, 2002
Performed by Underworld on the album *A Hundred Days Off* (V2,
    2002).

Two Wrongs
Words and music by Jerry Duplessis and Wyclef Jean
Huss Zwingli Publishing, 2002/Sony ATV Tunes LLC, 2002
Performed by Wyclef Jean featuring Claudia Ortiz on the album
    Masquerade (Columbia, 2002).

U

U Don't Have to Call
Words and music by Charles Hugo and Pharrell Williams
Chase Chad Music, 2001/EMI-April Music, 2001/EMI-Blackwood
  Music, 2001/Waters of Nazareth Publishing, 2001
Performed by Usher on the album *8701* (Universal, 2001). Won a
  Grammy Award for Best Male R&B Vocal Performance, 2002.

Uh Huh
Words and music by Thabiso Nkhereanye, Christopher Stewart, Malik
  Crawford, Lil Fizz (pseudonym for Frederic Dreux), Traci Hale, and J
  Boog (pseudonym for Jarrell Houston)
Hitco South, 2002/Marchninenth Music, 2002/Morningside Trail Music,
  2002/Songs of Peer, 2002/Tabulous Music, 2002/Hale Yeah Music,
  2002/Peertunes LTD, 2002
Performed by B2K on the album *B2K* (Epic, 2002). Originally appeared
  on the soundtrack album *The New Guy* (Sony, 2001).

Unbroken
Words and music by Mary Lamar and Annie Roboff
Almo Music, 2001/Anwa Music, 2001/Platinum Plow, 2001/WB Music,
  2001
Performed by Tim McGraw on the album *Set This Circus Down* (Curb,
  2001).

Underneath It All
Words and music by Gwen Stefani and Dave Stewart
Universal-MCA Music Publishing, 2001/World of the Dolphin Music,
  2001/Careers-BMG Music Publishing, 2001
Performed by No Doubt featuring Lady Saw on the album *Rock Steady*
  (Interscope 2001).

Underneath Your Clothes
Words and music by Shakira Mebarak and Lester Mendez
Aniwi Music, 2001/Apollinaire Music, 2001/EMI-Blackwood Music,

2001/Sony/ATV Latin Music Publishing, 2001
Performed by Shakira on the album *Laundry Service* (Sony, 2001).

Up All Night
Words and music by Scott Russo
Unwritten Music, 2002
Performed by Unwritten Law on the album *Elva* (Interscope, 2002).

V

Vanilla Sky
Words and music by Paul McCartney
MPL Communications, 2001
Performed by Paul McCartney on the soundtrack album *Vanilla Sky*
(Warner Bros., 2001). Nominated for a Grammy Award, Best Song
Written for a Motion Picture/Television, 2002.

Viviendo
Words and music by Mark Anthony (pseudonym for Mark Muniz),
Fernando Osorio, and Jorge Villamizar
Sony Tunes, 2001/Fernando Osorio Songs, 2001/Warner-Tamerlane
Publishing, 2001
Performed by Marc Anthony on the album *Libre* (Columbia, 2001).

W

Waitin' for You
Words and music by Bob Dylan (pseudonym for Robert Zimmerman)
Special Rider Music, 2002
Performed by Bob Dylan on the soundtrack album *Divine Secrets of the Ya-Ya Sisterhood* (Sony, 2002).

Walk On
Words and music by Bono (pseudonym for Paul Hewson), music by The Edge (pseudonym for David Evans), Larry Mullen, Jr., and Adam Clayton
Universal Polygram International Pub., 2000
Performed by U2 on the album *America: A Tribute to Heroes* (Interscope, 2001). Originally performed by U2 on the album *All That You Can't Leave Behind* (Interscope, 2000). Nominated for a Grammy Award, Best Rock Performance by a Duo or Group With Vocal, 2002.

Walking Away
Words and music by Craig David and Mark Hill
WB Music, 2002/Music of Windswept, 2002
Performed by Craig David on the album *Born to Do It* (Atlantic, 2002).

Wanksta
Words and music by John Freeman and 50 Cent (pseudonym for Curtis Jackson)
Hidden Scrolls Publishing, 2002/Universal Music Publishing, 2002
Performed by 50 Cent on the soundtrack album *8 Mile* (Interscope, 2002).

Warning
Words and music by Brandon Boyd, Michael Einziger, Alex Katunich, Christopher Kilmore, and Jose Pasillas
EMI-April Music, 2001/Hunglikeyora, 2001
Performed by Incubus on the album *Morning View* (Sony, 2001).

Wasting My Time
Words and music by David Benedict, Daniel Craig, Jeremy Hora, and
    Dallas Smith
EMI-Blackwood Music, 2001/Default Productions, 2001
Performed by Default on the album *The Fallout* (TVT, 2001).

Way of Life
Words and music by William Bryan, Lil' Wayne (pseudonym for
    Dwayne Carter), Francine Golde, Duane Hitchings, Dennis Lambert,
    and Terrance Quaites
EMI-April Music, 2002/Sony ATV Tunes LLC, 2002/Strictly TQ Music,
    2002/Money Mack Music, 2002
Performed by Lil' Wayne on the album *500 Degreez* (Cash Money,
    2002).

We Are All Made of Stars
Words and music by Moby (pseudonym for Richard Hall)
Little Idiot Music, 2002/Warner-Tamerlane Publishing, 2002
Performed by Moby on the album *18* (V2, 2002).

We Thuggin'
Words and music by Fat Joe (pseudonym for Joseph Cartagena), Ronald
    Bowser, and R. Kelly (pseudonym for Steven Williams)
Joseph Cartagena Music, 2001/EMI-Blackwood Music, 2001/R. Kelly
    Music, 2001/Ron G Music, 2001/Zomba Songs, 2001
Performed by Fat Joe featuring R. Kelly on the album *Jealous Ones Still
    Envy (J.O.S.E.)* (Atlantic, 2001).

The Weakness in Me
Words and music by Joan Armatrading
Irving Music, 1981/Rondo Music London (PRS), 1981
Covered by Melissa Etheridge on the DVD *Live and Alone* (Universal,
    2002.) Originally performed by Joan Armatrading on the album *Walk
    Under Ladders* (A&M, 1981). Nominated for a Grammy Award, Best
    Female Rock Vocal Performance, 2002.

Welcome to Atlanta
Words and music by Ludacris (pseudonym for Christopher Bridges),
    Jalil Hutchins, Jermaine Dupri (pseudonym for Jermaine Mauldin),
    Christine Perren, Frederick Perren, and Lawrence Smith
EMI-April Music, 2001/Jobete Music, 2001/Ludacris Music Publishing,
    2001/Shania Cymone Music, 2001/Zomba Enterprises, 2001
Performed by Jermaine Dupri and Ludacris on the album *Instructions*
    (So So Def, 2001).

What About Us
Words and music by LaShawn Daniels, Freddie Jerkins, Rodney Jerkins,
    Nora Payne, and Kenisha Pratt

EMI-April Music, 2001/EMI-Blackwood Music, 2001/Ensign Music,
2001/Fred Jerkins Publishing, 2001/Generation 3rd Music, 2001/
Rodney Jerkins Productions, 2001/Songs of Windswept Pacific, 2001/
TTARP Music Publishing, 2001
Performed by Brandy on the album *Full Moon* (Atlantic, 2002).

What Does It Feel Like?
Words and music by Felix da Housecat (pseudonym for Felix Stallings)
Sherlock Holmes Music Ltd., 2001
Performed by Felix da Housecat on the album *Excursions* (Obsessive,
2002). Originally appeared on the album *Kittenz and Thee Glitz*
(Emperor Norton, 2001).

What If She's an Angel
Words and music by Bryan Wayne
Care Taker Music, 2002/Sony ATV Tree Publishing, 2002
Performed by Tommy Shane Steiner on the album *Then Came the Night*
(RCA, 2002).

What We're All About (Original Version)
Words and music by Dave Baksh, Steve Jocz, and Dreyck Whibley
Chrysalis Music, 2002/EMI-April Music, 2002/New Columbia Pictures
Music, 2002
Performed by Sum 41 on the soundtrack album *Spider-Man* (Columbia,
2002).

What a Wonderful World
Words and music by George Douglas (pseudonym for Robert Thiele)
and George Weiss
Abilene Music, 1967/Quartet Music, 1967/Range Road Music, 1967
Covered by Joey Ramone on the album *Don't Worry About Me*
(Sanctuary, 2002). Originally performed by Louis Armstrong.

What a Wonderful World
Words and music by George Douglas (pseudonym for Robert Thiele)
and George Weiss
Abilene Music, 1967/Quartet Music, 1967/Range Road Music, 1967
Covered by Tony Bennett featuring k.d. lang on the album *A Wonderful
World* (RPM/Columbia, 2002). Originally performed by Louis
Armstrong. Nominated for a Grammy Award, Best Pop Collaboration
With Vocals, 2002.

Whatchulookinat
Words and music by Whitney Houston, Jerry Muhammad, Andre Lewis,
and Tammie Harris
Nippy Music, 2002/Dangerous & Legit Publishing, 2002
Performed by Whitney Houston on the album *Just Whitney* (Arista,
2002).

What's Going On
Words and music by Renaldo Benson, Alfred Cleveland, and Marvin
  Gaye
FCG Music, 1970/Jobete Music, 1970/M G III Music, 1970/NMG
  Music, 1970/Stone Agate Music, 1970
Covered by Chaka Khan and the Funk Brothers on the soundtrack
  album *Standing in the Shadows of Motown* (Hip-O, 2002). Originally
  performed by Marvin Gaye on the album *What's Going On* (Motown,
  1971). Won a Grammy Award for Best Traditional R&B Vocal
  Performance, 2002.

What's Golden?
Words and music by James Boxley, Dante Givens, Courtenay
  Henderson, Lucas MacFadden, Mark Potsic, Carlton Ridenhour, Eric
  Sadler, Marc Stuart, and Charles Stewart
DJ Nu Mark Music, 2002/Reach Global Songs, 2002/Songs of
  Universal, 2002/Your Mother's Music, 2002
Performed by Jurassic 5 on the album *Power in Numbers* (Interscope,
  2002).

What's Luv?
Words and music by Ja Rule (pseudonym for Jeffrey Atkins), Fat Joe
  (pseudonym for Joseph Cartagena), Irv Gotti (pseudonym for Irving
  Lorenzo), Andre Parker, and Christopher Rios
DJ Irv Publishing, 2001/Ensign Music, 2001/Slavery Music, 2001/Songs
  of Universal, 2001/Famous Music, 2001/Soldierz Touch, 2001/Joseph
  Cartagena Music, 2001/White Rhino Music, 2001/Universal Music
  Publishing, 2001
Performed by Fat Joe featuring Ashanti on the album *Jealous Ones Still
  Envy (J.O.S.E.)* (Atlantic, 2001). Nominated for a Grammy Award,
  Best Rap/Sung Collaboration, 2002.

What's Your Flava
Words and music by Craig David, Trevor Henry, and Anthony Marshall
BMG Songs, 2002/Music of Windswept, 2002
Performed by Craig David on the album *Slicker Than Your Average*
  (Atlantic, 2002).

When I'm Gone
Words and music by Bradley Arnold, Robert Harrell, Christopher
  Henderson, and Matthew Roberts
Escatawpa Songs, 2002/Universal Songs of Polygram Intntl., 2002
Performed by 3 Doors Down on the album *Away From the Sun*
  (Universal, 2002). Nominated for Grammy Awards, Best Rock
  Performance by a Duo or Group With Vocal, 2002, and Best Rock
  Song, 2002.

When the Last Time
Words and music by Charles Hugo, Malice (pseudonym for Gene Thornton), Pusha T (pseudonym for Terrence Thornton), and Pharrell Williams
Chase Chad Music, 2002/EMI-April Music, 2002/Gemarc, 2002/ Terrardome Music, 2002/EMI-Blackwood Music, 2002/Waters of Nazareth Publishing, 2002
Performed by Clipse on the album *Lord Willin'* (Arista, 2002).

When You Lie Next to Me
Words and music by Kellie Coffey, Martin Derstine, and Trina Harmon
Kelodies, 2002/Lillywilly Music, 2002/Platinum Plow, 2002/WB Music, 2002
Performed by Kellie Coffey on the album *When You Lie Next to Me* (BNA, 2002).

When You're on Top
Words and music by Jakob Dylan
EMI-April Music, 2002/Tear It Down Music, 2002
Performed by the Wallflowers on the album *Red Letter Days* (Interscope, 2002).

Where Are You Going
Words and music by Dave Matthews
Colden Grey Ltd., 2002
Performed by the Dave Matthews Band on the soundtrack album *Mr. Deeds* (RCA, 2002). Song also appears on the album *Busted Stuff* (RCA, 2002). Nominated for a Grammy Award, Best Pop Performance by a Duo or Group With Vocal, 2002.

Where Do We Go From Here
Words and music by Eugene Lenardo and Richard Patrick
EMI-April Music, 2002/Happy Ditties from Paradise, 2002
Performed by Filter on the album *The Amalgamut* (Warner Bros., 2002).

Where Were You (When the World Stopped Turning)
Words and music by Alan Jackson
EMI-April Music, 2001/Tri Angels Music, 2001
Performed by Alan Jackson on the album *Drive* (Arista, 2002). Won a Grammy Award for Best Country Song, 2002. Nominated for Grammy Awards, Best Male Country Vocal Performance, 2002, and Song of the Year, 2002.

Where Would You Be
Words and music by Rick Ferrell and Rachel Proctor
Castle Street, Nashville, 2001/Mr. Noise Music, 2001/Warner-Tamerlane Publishing, 2001

Performed by Martina McBride on the album *Greatest Hits* (RCA, 2001).

Where's Your Head At?

Words and music by Felix Buxton, Simon Ratcliffe, and Gary Numan (pseudonym for Gary Webb)

Songs of Universal, 2001/Universal MCA Music Ltd., 2001/Universal Music Publishing Int. Ltd., 2001

Performed by Basement Jaxx on the soundtrack album *Lara Croft: Tomb Raider* (Elektra/Asylum 2001). Originally appeared on Basement Jaxx's album *Rooty* (Astralwerks, 2001).

Wherever You Will Go

Words and music by Alex Band and Aaron Kamin

Alex Band Music, 2001/Amedeo Music, 2001/Careers-BMG Music Publishing, 2001

Performed by the Calling on the album *Camino Palmero* (RCA, 2001).

White America

Words and music by Eminem (pseudonym for Marshall Mathers), Jeffrey Bass, Steve King, and Luis Resto

Eight Mile Style Music, 2002/Ensign Music, 2002

Performed by Eminem on the album *The Eminem Show* (Aftermath/Interscope, 2002).

The Whole World

Words by Dre (pseudonym for Andre Benjamin), Big Boi (pseudonym for Antwan Patton), and David Sheats, words and music by Killer Mike (pseudonym for Michael Render)

Aniyah's Music, 2001/Chrysalis Music, 2001/Dungeon Rat Music, 2001/Gnat Booty Music, 2001

Performed by Outkast featuring Killer Mike on the album *Big Boi and Dre Present. . . Outkast* (LaFace, 2001). Won a Grammy Award for Best Rap Performance by a Duo or Group, 2002.

Who's Your Daddy?

Words and music by Toby Keith (pseudonym for Toby Covel)

Tokeco Tunes, 2002

Performed by Toby Keith on the album *Unleashed* (DreamWorks, 2002).

Why Aye Man

Words and music by Mark Knopfler

Will Decide Ltd., 2002

Performed by Mark Knopfler on the album *The Ragpicker's Dream* (Warner Bros., 2002).

Why Don't We Fall in Love

Words and music by Rich Harrison

EMI-Blackwood Music, 2002/Vice Game Music, 2002
Performed by Amerie on the album *All I Have* (Rise/Columbia, 2002).

Will the Circle Be Unbroken (Glory, Glory)
Words and music by A.P. Carter
Peer International Corp., 1979/Big Toots Tunes, 1979
Performed by Nitty Gritty Dirt Band featuring Taj Mahal, Alison
  Krauss, and Doc Watson on the album *Will the Circle Be Unbroken,
  Vol III* (Capitol, 2002). Originally performed by the Carter Family.
  Nominated for a Grammy Award, Best Country Collaboration With
  Vocals, 2002.

Wish I Didn't Miss You, also known as I Wish I Didn't Miss You Anymore
Words and music by Leon Huff, Andrea Martin, Ivan Matias, Gene
  McFadden, and John Whitehead
Ghetto Fabulous Entertainment, 2002/God's Crying Publishing, 2002/
  Sony ATV Tunes LLC, 2002/Mijac Music, 2002/Warner-Tamerlane
  Publishing, 2002
Performed by Angie Stone on the album *Mahogany Soul* (J, 2001).

Without Me
Words and music by Eminem (pseudonym for Marshall Mathers),
  Jeffrey Bass, Kevin Bell, Malcolm McLaren, Trevor Horn, and Anne
  Dudley
Bughouse, 2002/Eight Mile Style Music, 2002/Ensign Music, 2002/Nuez
  Music, 2002/Reach Global Songs, 2002/Satisfaction Fulfilled Ltd.
  (PRS), 2002/Buffalo Music Factory, 2002
Performed by Eminem on the album *The Eminem Show* (Interscope,
  2002). Won a Grammy Award for Best Short Form Music Video,
  2002. Nominated for Grammy Awards, Best Male Rap Solo
  Performance, 2002, and Record of the Year, 2002.

Work It
Words and music by Melissa Elliott, DMC (pseudonym for Darryl
  McDaniels), Timbaland (pseudonym for Timothy Mosley), Run
  (pseudonym for Joseph Simmons), and Paul Simon
Mass Confusion Productions, 2002/Rush Groove Records, 2002/Virginia
  Beach Music, 2002/WB Music, 2002
Performed by Missy Elliott on the album *Under Construction* (Elektra,
  2002).

Work It Out
Words and music by Charles Hugo, Beyonce Knowles, and Pharrell
  Williams
Beyonce Publishing, 2002/Chase Chad Music, 2002/EMI-April Music,
  2002

Performed by Beyonce Knowles on the soundtrack album *Austin Powers in Goldmember* (Maverick, 2002).

Work in Progress
Words and music by Alan Jackson
EMI-April Music, 2002/Tri Angels Music, 2002
Performed by Alan Jackson on the album *Drive* (Arista, 2002).

The World's Greatest
Words and music by R. Kelly (pseudonym for Steven Williams)
Zomba Songs, 2001/R. Kelly Music, 2001
Performed by R. Kelly on the soundtrack album *Ali* (Interscope, 2001).
    Nominated for a Grammy Award, Best Male R&B Vocal
    Performance, 2002.

Wrapped Around
Words and music by Brad Paisley, John Lovelace, and Charles DuBois
EMI-April Music, 2001/Love Ranch Music, 2001/Sea Gayle Music,
    2001
Performed by Brad Paisley on the album *Part II* (Arista, 2001).

Y

Y Tu Te Vas
Words and music by Franco De Vita
WB Music, 2002
Performed by Chayanne on the album *Grandes Exitos* (Sony Discos, 2002).

Yes
Words and music by Rick Nowels, William Steinberg, and Marie D'Ubaldo
Jerk Awake Music, Los Angeles, 2002/EMI-April Music, 2002/Future Furniture, 2002/Hit & Run Music Publishing, 2002
Performed by Amber on the album *Naked* (Tommy Boy, 2002).

You Can't Go Home Again!
Words and music by DJ Shadow (pseudonym for Josh Davis)
Universal Music Publishing, 2002
Performed by DJ Shadow on the album *The Private Press* (MCA, 2002).

You Give Me Something
Words and music by Nick Fyffe, Rob Harris, and Jason Kay
EMI-Blackwood Music, 2001/EMI Music Publishing Ltd., 2001
Performed by Jamiroquai on the album *A Funk Odyssey* (Epic, 2001).

You Know That I Love You
Words and music by Chris Absolam, Walter Hawkins, and Richard Smith
Jamie Hawkins Publishers, 2001/Sony ATV Songs LLC, 2001/Noel Absolam Music, 2001/Richard Smith Publishing, 2001
Performed by Donell Jones on the album *Life Goes On* (LaFace, 2002).

You Know You're Right
Words and music by Kurt Cobain
EMI-Virgin Songs, 2002/End of Music, 2002
Performed by Nirvana on the album *Nirvana* (DGC, 2002).

You Make Me Sick
Words and music by Obi Nwobosi, Ainsworth Prasad, and Mark Tabb
Wood Fella Muzic Publishing, London, England, 2000/Ainzworth Amill
   Music, 2000/E Two Music, 2000/EMI-April Music, 2000/Me and
   Chuma Music, 2000
Performed by Pink on the album *Can't Take Me Home* (LaFace, 2000).

You Never Met a Motherf**ker Quite Like Me
Words and music by Allen Collins, Kid Rock (pseudonym for Robert
   Ritchie), and Ronald VanZant
EMI Longitude Music, 2001/Thirty Two Mile Music, 2001/Universal
   Duchess Music, 2001/Warner-Tamerlane Publishing, 2001
Performed by Kid Rock on the album *Cocky* (Atlantic, 2001).

You Should Be Here, see **Be Here.**

Young
Words and music by Steven McEwan, Naoise Sheridan, and Craig
   Wiseman
Careers-BMG Music Publishing, 2002/BMG Songs, 2002/Mrs.
   Lumpkin's Poodle, 2002
Performed by Kenny Chesney on the album *No Shoes, No Shirt, No
   Problems* (BNA, 2002).

Your Body Is a Wonderland
Words and music by John Mayer
Sony Tunes, 2000/Specific Harm Music, 2000
Performed by John Mayer on the album *Room for Squares* (Columbia,
   2001). Won a Grammy Award for Best Male Pop Vocal Performance,
   2002.

Youth of the Nation
Words and music by Noah Bernardo, Marcos Curiel, Mark Daniels, and
   Paul Sandoval
Famous Music, 2001/Souljah Music, 2001
Performed by P.O.D. on the album *Satellite* (Atlantic, 2001). Nominated
   for a Grammy Award, Best Hard Rock Performance, 2002.

Z

The Zephyr Song
Words and music by Flea (pseudonym for Michael Balzary), John
  Frusciante, Anthony Kiedis, and Chad Smith
Moebetoblame Music, 2002
Performed by Red Hot Chili Peppers on the album *By the Way* (Warner
  Bros., 2002).

Lyricists & Composers Index

Lyricists & Composers Index

Lyricists & Composers Index

Lyricists & Composers Index

Lyricists & Composers Index

Lyricists & Composers Index

Gate, Larry
  Crush Tonight
Gaye, Marvin
  What's Going On
George, Sergio
  La Negra Tiene Tumbao
George, Tokiko
  Still Not Over You
Gerrard, Matthew
  Help Me
Gervais, Stephane
  My Plague
Gibbs, Douglas
  Song Cry
Gilbert, Chad
  Head on Collision
  My Friends Over You
Giles, Cameron
  Hey Ma
  Oh Boy
Gilmore, Jimmie Dale
  South Wind of Summer
Gist, Keir
  Anything
  Fabulous
Givens, Dante
  What's Golden?
Glan, Lucia
  Por Ese Hombre
Goercke, Chris
  Shut Up
Golde, Francine
  Way of Life
Goldenberg, Mark
  The Night Inside Me
Goldenthal, Elliot
  Burn It Blue
Goldowitz, Paul
  Barenaked
Goldsmith, Jerrald
  If We Could Remember
Gomez, Escolar
  Si Tu Te Vas
Goodman, Donald
  Ol' Red
Goodwin, Jamie
  There Goes the Fear

Gordon, Allen
  Feels Good (Don't Worry Bout a
    Thing)
Gordon, Allen, Jr.
  Let's Stay Home Tonight
Gordon, Kim
  The Empty Page
Gore, Martin
  Freelove
Gotti, Irv
  Ain't It Funny
  Always on Time
  Baby
  Diary
  Down A** B**ch
  Down 4 U
  Foolish
  Happy
  Opposites Attract (What They Like)
  Rainy Dayz
  What's Luv?
Graffin, Greg
  Supersonic
Grant, Colyn
  Move It Like This
Gray, Chad
  Not Falling
Gray, David
  The Other Side
  Silver Lining
Gray, James
  Break You Off
Gray, Ling
  Right Here, Right Now
Gray, Paul
  My Plague
Gray, Shari
  Hush Lil' Lady
Gray, Terius *see* Juvenile
Green, Pat
  Three Days
Greenberg, Steve
  Move It Like This
Greenwood, Lee
  God Bless the U.S.A.
Gregson, John
  Let It Rain
Griffin, William *see* Rakim

Lyricists & Composers Index

Lyricists & Composers Index

Lyricists & Composers Index

Lyricists & Composers Index

Lyricists & Composers Index

Lyricists & Composers Index

Lyricists & Composers Index

Important Performances Index

Songs are listed under the works in which they were introduced or given significant renditions. The index is organized into major sections by performance medium: Album, Movie, Musical, Performer, Revue, Television Show.

Album

Important Performances Index — Album

Important Performances Index — Album

Important Performances Index — Performer

Awards Index

A list of songs nominated for Academy Awards by the Academy of Motion Picture Arts and Sciences and Grammy Awards from the National Academy of Recording Arts and Sciences. Asterisks indicate the winners; multiple listings indicate multiple nominations.

2002

Academy Award
  Burn It Blue
  Father and Daughter
  The Hands That Built America
  I Move On
  Lose Yourself*
Grammy Award
  Aeriels
  All My Life
  All My Life*
  All the Way
  Alone
  Always on Time
  Any Day Now
  Apollo
  Approaching Pavonis Mons by Balloon
    (Utopia Planitia)*
  As It Is
  Auld Lang Syne*
  The Barry Williams Show
  Be Here
  Bear Mountain Hop
  Bearing Straight
  Beautiful Mess
  Better Than Anything
  Blackbird
  Blessed

Bouncin' Back (Bumpin' Me Against
    the Wall)
Bridge Over Troubled Water
Christmas Song
Complicated
Cry*
Dagger Through the Heart
Darkness, Darkness
Days Go By
Days Go By*
Diary
Dilemma
Dilemma*
Dirrty
Don't Know Why*
Don't Mess With My Man
18
The Essence
Everyday
Flesh and Blood
Floetic
Foolish
45
Fragile
The Game of Love*
Get Inside
Get the Party Started
Gettin' Grown

List of Publishers

A directory of publishers of the songs included in *Popular Music, 2002*. Publishers that are members of the American Society of Composers, Authors, and Publishers or whose catalogs are available under ASCAP license are indicated by the designation (ASCAP). Publishers that have granted performing rights to Broadcast Music, Inc., are designated by the notation (BMI). Publishers whose catalogs are represented by The Society of Composers, Authors and Music Publishers of Canada, are indicated by the designation (SOCAN). Publishers whose catalogs are represented by SESAC, Inc., are indicated by the designation (SESAC).

The addresses were gleaned from a variety of sources, including ASCAP, BMI, SOCAN, SESAC, and *Billboard* magazine. As in any volatile industry, many of the addresses may become outdated quickly. In the interim between the book's completion and its subsequent publication, some publishers may have been consolidated into others or changed hands. This is a fact of life long endured by the music business and its constituents. The data collected here, and throughout the book, are as accurate as such circumstances allow.

A

Abilene Music (ASCAP)
c/o Songwriters Guild
1500 Harbor Blvd.
Weehawken, New Jersey 07087

ABKCO Music (BMI)
1700 Broadway
New York, New York 10019-5905

Absinthe Music (BMI)
see Warner-Chappell Music

Noel Absolam Music (ASCAP)
1026 E. 100
Brooklyn, New York 11236

Acuff Rose Music Publishing (BMI)
65 Music Square West
Nashville, Tennessee 37203-3207

Adria K Music (ASCAP)
see Wixen Music Publishing

Aerostation Corp. (ASCAP)
see Universal-MCA Music Publishing

AFRT Music (ASCAP)
c/o Ariass Fortune Inc.
P.O. Box 6590
Beverly Hills, California 90212

List of Publishers

Aggressive Music (ASCAP)
see Universal-MCA Music Publishing

Ah Choo Music (ASCAP)
see Universal-MCA Music Publishing

Ain't Nothing but Funkin' Music (ASCAP)
c/o Provident Financial Management
10345 W. Olympic Blvd., #200
Los Angeles, California 90064

Ainzworth Amill Music (ASCAP)
see EMI Music Publishing

Air Control Music (ASCAP)
see EMI Music Publishing

Mitch Albom Music
Address Unavailable

Alex Band Music (BMI)
Address Unavailable

Almo/Irving
1358 N. LaBrea
Los Angeles, California 90028

Almo Music (ASCAP)
2440 Sepulveda Blvd.
Ste. 1119
Los Angeles, California 90064

Amedeo Music (BMI)
Address Unavailable

American Broadcasting Music (ASCAP)
30 W. 67th St., 9th Fl.
New York, New York 10023

Andrew WK Music (BMI)
see Universal-MCA Music Publishing

Angel Pie Publishing (BMI)
Address Unavailable

Animal Fair (ASCAP)
see Famous Music

Aniwi Music (BMI)
Address Unavailable

Aniyah's Music (ASCAP)
2615 Collier Dr., NW
Atlanta, Georgia 30318

Anne-Rachel Music (ASCAP)
see Warner-Chappell Music

Annotation Music (ASCAP)
see Warner-Chappell Music

Anwa Music (ASCAP)
see Almo Music

Aphrodite Music (ASCAP)
c/o Eastman & Eastman
39 W. 54th St.
New York, New York 10019

Apollinaire Music (BMI)
2510 SW 105 Ct.
Miami, Florida 33165-2529

April Blue Music (ASCAP)
see EMI Music Publishing

ARC Music (BMI)
254 West 54th St., 13th Fl.
New York, New York 10019

Arm Your Dillo
Address Unavailable

Arte Humane (ASCAP)
see Peermusic Ltd.

Artmob Music (BMI)
10231 Pinehurst Dr.
Austin, Texas 78747

Ascent Music Inc. (BMI)
c/o Logan H. Westbrooks
1902 5th Ave.
Los Angeles, California 90018

Aurelius Publishing (ASCAP)
see Aphrodite Music

B

B. Shaw Publishing (ASCAP)
475 Lenox Ave., #3C
New York, New York 10037

B Springs Publishing (ASCAP)
c/o J.D. Dallam
310 Pavonia Ave.
Jersey City, New York 07302

Baby Paul Muzik (BMI)
c/o The Royalty Network
224 West 30th St., Ste. 1007
New York, New York 10001

Babyboys Little Pub Co (SESAC)
see Warner-Chappell Music

Bachus Music (BMI)
see Lastrada Music

Bacteria Music (ASCAP)
see Wixen Music Publishing

Bad Alter Boy Music (BMI)
c/o Kaplan Corp.
9454 Wilshire Blvd., Ste. 711
Beverly Hills, California 90212

Barely Breathing (ASCAP)
see EMI Music Publishing

Barland Music (BMI)
see Bug Music

Base Pipe Music (ASCAP)
see Warner-Chappell Music

Bases Loaded Music (ASCAP)
see BMG Songs

Beanly Songs (BMI)
see Sony ATV Tunes LLC

Beavers Brand Music (ASCAP)
c/o MCS Music America Inc.
1625 Broadway, 4th Fl.
Nashville, Tennessee 37203

Bee Mo Easy Music (ASCAP)
see EMI Music Publishing

Irving Berlin Music (ASCAP)
1065 Avenue of the Americas
Ste. 2400
New York, New York 10018

Bernard's Other Music (BMI)
see Warner-Chappell Music

Berns II Music Publishing (BMI)
see Sony ATV Tunes LLC

Beyonce Publishing (ASCAP)
c/o Music World Entertainment
1505 Hadley St.
Houston, Texas 77002

Beyond the Beat Publishing (BMI)
Address Unavailable

Bhaji Maker (ASCAP)
see Peermusic Ltd.

Bicycle Spanaird Music (BMI)
c/o Kaplan Corp.
9454 Wilshire Blvd., Ste. 711
Beverly Hills, California 90212

Bidnis (BMI)
c/o Stuart Ditsky CPA
733 Third Ave., 19th Fl.
New York, New York 10017

Big Ass Pete (ASCAP)
see EMI Music Publishing

Big Caboose Music (ASCAP)
see BMG Songs

Big Elk Music (ASCAP)
c/o Don Williams Music Group
16760 Escalan Dr.
Encino Hills, California 91436

Big Herb's Music (BMI)
225 Cornwell Dr.
Bear, Delaware 19701

Big Purple Dog (ASCAP)
see Sony ATV Tunes LLC

Big Red Tractor Music (ASCAP)
1503 17th Ave. South
Nashville, Tennessee 37212

List of Publishers

Big Toots Tunes
c/o S. Turner & Co.
8383 Wilshire Blvd., Ste. 616
Beverly Hills, California 90211

Big Yellow Dog Music (BMI)
see Sony ATV Tunes LLC

Bill-Lee Music (BMI)
c/o Williams Nichols
233 W. 99th St., Apt. 5E
New York, New York 10025-5016

Black Bull Music (ASCAP)
4616 Magnolia Blvd.
Burbank, California 91505

Black Fountain Music (ASCAP)
see EMI Music Publishing

Black Lava (ASCAP)
see Universal-MCA Music Publishing

Black Shadow Records (ASCAP)
2111 NW 139th St., Ste. 14
Miami, Florida 33054

Blakemore Avenue Music (ASCAP)
2004 Wedgewood Ave.
Nashville, Tennessee 37212

Blanco Meow Music (SESAC)
see Universal-MCA Music Publishing

Blitz Package Music (BMI)
c/o The Royalty Network
224 West 30th St., Ste. 1007
New York, New York 10001

Block off Broad Publishing (BMI)
Address Unavailable

Blondie Rockwell Music (ASCAP)
see Universal-MCA Music Publishing

Blotter Music (ASCAP)
see Windswept Pacific Entertainment

Blue Haze Music (ASCAP)
10865 Bluffside Dr., #211
Studio City, California 91604

Blue's Baby Music (ASCAP)
see Universal-MCA Music Publishing

Blunts Guns and Funds (ASCAP)
see Famous Music

BMG Music (ASCAP)
1540 Broadway
New York, New York 10036

BMG Music Publishing Ltd.
Address Unavailable

BMG Songs (ASCAP)
8750 Wilshire Blvd.
Beverly Hills, California 90211

Board Stiff Music (BMI)
Address Unavailable

Boggy Bottom Publishing (ASCAP)
c/o VWC Management
13343 Bellevue Redmond Rd.
Bellevue, Washington 98005

Bon Jovi Publishing (ASCAP)
see Universal-MCA Music Publishing

Bonedaddy's Publishing (BMI)
304 Braeswood Rd.
Austin, Texas 78704-7200

Bossy Pants Music (BMI)
Address Unavailable

Bourne Co. (ASCAP)
c/o Ms. Beebe Bourne
5 West 37th St., 6th Fl.
New York, New York 10018

Bobby Boyd Music (BMI)
c/o Copyright Mgmt. International
1625 Broadway, 4th Fl.
Nashville, Tennessee 37203

The Braids Publishing (ASCAP)
see Zomba Enterprises

Bright Gray Publishing (ASCAP)
see EMI Music Publishing

Bro N' Sis Music (BMI)
c/o Carlin America, Inc.
126 East 38th St.
New York, New York 10016

Brandon Brody Music (BMI)
see Warner-Chappell Music

Bucks Music Ltd.
Address Unavailable

Buffalo Music Factory (BMI)
1824 S. Point View St.
Los Angeles, California 90035-4624

Bug Music (BMI)
1645 N. Vine St., Penthouse
Hollywood, California 90028

Bughouse (ASCAP)
see Bug Music

Bull's Creek Publishing (BMI)
P.O. Box 330519
Nashville, Tennessee 37203-7504

Buna Boy Music (BMI)
P.O. Box 50314
Nashville, Tennessee 37205

Butterman Land Publishing (BMI)
see Universal-MCA Music Publishing

Buzzard Rock Music (BMI)
see Bug Music

C

Cagey Music Publishing (BMI)
650 Gates Ave., Apt. 3G
Brooklyn, New York 11221-1735

Cal IV Entertainment (ASCAP)
c/o Daniel Hill
808 19th Ave. South
Nashville, Tennessee 37203

Cancelled Lunch Music (ASCAP)
see Universal-MCA Music Publishing

Care Taker Music (BMI)
see Sony ATV Tunes LLC

Careers-BMG Music Publishing (BMI)
8750 Wilshire Blvd.
Beverly Hills, California 90211

Andreas Carlsson Publishing
Address Unavailable

Carnevalli Music
Address Unavailable

Joseph Cartagena Music (ASCAP)
see Jelly's Jams LLC Music

Cartoon Aroma Hand Music (ASCAP)
8360 Hollywood Blvd.
Los Angeles, California 90069

Castle Street (ASCAP)
1109 16th Ave. S.
Nashville, Tennessee 37212

Chase Chad Music (ASCAP)
see EMI Music Publishing

Cherry Lane Music (ASCAP)
6 E. 32nd St., 11th Fl.
New York, New York 10016

Cherry River Music (BMI)
6 East 32nd St., 11th Fl.
New York, New York 10016

Chi-Boy Music (ASCAP)
see Wixen Music Publishing

Ching Music (ASCAP)
see Peermusic Ltd.

Chitty Chitty Music (ASCAP)
4350 B 136th St.
Hawthorne, California 90250

Chops Not Chaps Music (BMI)
see Bug Music

Jaedon Christopher Publishing (ASCAP)
c/o Grubman, Indursky, & Schindler
152 West 57th St.
New York, New York 10019

Chrysalis Music (ASCAP)
8500 Melrose, 2nd Fl.
Los Angeles, California 90069

List of Publishers

Chrysalis Songs (BMI)
see Chrysalis Music

Chuck Wagon Gourmet Music (ASCAP)
see Famous Music

Chyna Baby Music (BMI)
see EMI Music Publishing

Marie Claire Music (ASCAP)
340 Montross Ave.
Peekskill, New York 10566

Coburn Music (BMI)
33 Music Square West, Ste. 110
Nashville, Tennessee 37203-3226

Code Word Nemesis (ASCAP)
120 NE State St., No. 418
Olympia, Washington 98501

Cold Chillin' Music (ASCAP)
see Warner-Chappell Music

Colden Grey Ltd. (ASCAP)
c/o Red Light Management
P.O. Box 1911
Charlottesville, Virginia 22903

Colgems EMI Music (ASCAP)
see EMI Music Publishing

Janice Combs Music (BMI)
see EMI Music Publishing

Justin Combs Publishing (ASCAP)
see EMI Music Publishing

Connotation Music (BMI)
see Warner-Chappell Music

Coptic Soundsations Publishing (BMI)
c/o Soundsations Publishing
2271 Grand Ave.
Bronx, New York 10468

Copyright Control Music (BMI)
see Bug Music

Copyright Management Services (BMI)
1625 Broadway, 4th Fl.
Nashville, Tennessee 37203

Corner of Clark and Kent (ASCAP)
see EMI Music Publishing

Crack Rock Music (BMI)
P.O. Box 490387
Mt. Berry, Georgia 30149

Craig Beast Music
Address Unavailable

Creative Artists Agency (ASCAP)
see Chrysalis Music

Crited Music (BMI)
see Warner-Chappell Music

Cross Keys Publishing (ASCAP)
see Sony ATV Tunes LLC

Cross the Water Publishing (ASCAP)
c/o Frederick Tulloch
12445 NW 21 Court
Miami, Florida 33167

Cryptron Music (BMI)
see EMI Music Publishing

Mike Curb Music (ASCAP)
47 Music Square East
Nashville, Tennessee 37203

Cyanide Breathmint Music (ASCAP)
see BMG Music

Shania Cymone Music (ASCAP)
see EMI Music Publishing

Cyphercleff Music Publishing (ASCAP)
see EMI Music Publishing

Cyrillic Soup (ASCAP)
see Wixen Music Publishing

D

D Nico International (BMI)
1625 N. Laurel Ave., Ste. 10
Los Angeles, California 90046

Da Bess Music
Address Unavailable

Da Doo Da Publishing (SESAC)
c/o Pace
325 Nesconset Hwy.
Hauppauge, New York 11788-2522

Da Fabulous BeatBrokers Music
Address Unavailable

Daddy's Downstairs Again (ASCAP)
9365 Rollin Cresent
Brossard, Quebec J4X 2P8
Canada

Dakoda House (ASCAP)
see EMI Music Publishing

Dangerous & Legit Publishing
Address Unavailable

Danica Music (BMI)
2170 Commerce Ave., Ste. S
Concord, California 94520

Davince Music (BMI)
see Bug Music

Dayna's Day Publishing (BMI)
see Warner-Chappell Music

Ddevil Music (ASCAP)
see Sony ATV Tunes LLC

Def Jam Music (ASCAP)
see Universal-MCA Music Publishing

Default Productions
Address Unavailable

Demis Hot Songs (ASCAP)
see EMI Music Publishing

Demon of Screamin Music (ASCAP)
see EMI Music Publishing

Demonoid Deluxe Music (ASCAP)
see Warner-Chappell Music

Denson Filez Music (BMI)
c/o The Royalty Network
224 West 30th St., Ste. 1007
New York, New York 10001

Desmone Music (BMI)
see Sony ATV Tunes LLC

Desmundo Music (ASCAP)
c/o Desmobile Productions, Inc.
4045 Sheridan Ave., Ste. 256
Miami Beach, Florida 33140

Deston Songs (ASCAP)
see Sony ATV Tunes LLC

Dirty Dre Music (ASCAP)
see Universal-MCA Music Publishing

Dirty Shorts (ASCAP)
see Peermusic Ltd.

Disappearing One (ASCAP)
c/o VWC Management
13343 Bellevue-Redmond Rd.
Bellevue, Washington 98005

Walt Disney Music Co. (ASCAP)
see Disney Music Publishing

Disney Music Publishing (ASCAP)
500 S. Buena Vista St., MC 6174
Burbank, California 91521

Divided Music (BMI)
see Universal-MCA Music Publishing

Divine Mill Music (ASCAP)
see Warner-Chappell Music

Divine Pimp Publishing (ASCAP)
see BMG Songs

DJ Hi Tek Music Publishing (BMI)
see Windswept Pacific Entertainment

DJ Irv Publishing (BMI)
see Famous Music

DJ Nu Mark Music (BMI)
Address Unavailable

Donceno Music Publishing (ASCAP)
2541 7th Ave., Apt. 27C
New York, New York 10039

Door Number One Music
see Universal-MCA Music Publishing

List of Publishers

Dors-D Music (ASCAP)
    54 Boerum St., #16E
    Brooklyn, New York 11206

Dreaming Jewels Music
    Address Unavailable

Dreamworks Songs (ASCAP)
    c/o Dreamworks Music Publishing
    9268 W. 3rd St.
    Beverly Hills, California 90210

Drippin' Publishing (BMI)
    304 Braeswood Rd.
    Austin, Texas 78704-3130

Drop Your Pants Publishing (ASCAP)
    see Zomba Enterprises

Dungeon Rat Music (ASCAP)
    see EMI Music Publishing

Duro Music (BMI)
    see EMI Music Publishing

Dutchdaddy Music (ASCAP)
    c/o Crisis Management Inc.
    1288 West Laurelton Pkwy.
    Teaneck, New Jersey 07666

Dutty Rock Music (ASCAP)
    see EMI Music Publishing

Dynatone Publishing (BMI)
    see Warner-Chappell Music

E

E Two Music (ASCAP)
    see EMI Music Publishing

Earsnot Music (ASCAP)
    see Warner-Chappell Music

East New York Music (BMI)
    216 Sumpter St., Apt. 2
    Brooklyn, New York 11233

Ecaf Music (BMI)
    see Sony ATV Tunes LLC

Eddie F. Music (ASCAP)
    100 Piermont Rd.
    Closter, New Jersey 07624

800 Pound Gorilla Music (SESAC)
    c/o Paper Jam Music
    8075 West 3rd St., Ste. 400
    Los Angeles, California 90048-4319

Eight Mile Style Music (BMI)
    c/o Jeffrey Irwin Bass
    1525 East Nine Mile Rd.
    Ferndale, Michigan 48220

Eighteenth Letter Music (BMI)
    6 East 32nd St., 11th Fl.
    New York, New York 10016

Eiseman & Associates
    Address Unavailable

Ekop Publishing (BMI)
    see Sony ATV Tunes LLC

Elephant 6 Publishing (ASCAP)
    c/o The Elephant 6 Recording Co.
    2057 Rebel Rd.
    Lexington, Kentucky 40503

Eligible Music (PRS)
    Address Unavailable

Elliot/Jacobsen Music Publishing (ASCAP)
    P.O. Box 547
    Larkspur, California 94939

Elvis Mambo Music (ASCAP)
    see Music of Windswept

Embassy Music (BMI)
    257 Park Ave. South, 20th Fl.
    New York, New York 10010

EMI-April Music (ASCAP)
    see EMI Music Publishing

EMI-Blackwood Music (BMI)
    see EMI Music Publishing

EMI-Full Keel Music (ASCAP)
    see EMI Music Publishing

EMI Longitude Music (BMI)
see EMI Music Publishing

EMI Music Publishing
810 Seventh Ave.
New York, New York 10019

EMI Music Publishing Ltd.
Address Unavailable

EMI Unart Catalogue (BMI)
see EMI Music Publishing

EMI-Virgin Music (ASCAP)
see EMI Music Publishing

EMI-Virgin Songs (BMI)
see EMI Music Publishing

Encore Entertainment LLC (BMI)
121 17th Ave. South
Nashville, Tennessee 37203

End of Music (BMI)
see EMI Music Publishing

Enot Publishing (ASCAP)
see Sony ATV Tunes LLC

Ensign Music (BMI)
see Famous Music

Escatawpa Songs (BMI)
c/o Frascogna Courtney PLLC
P.O. Box 23126
Jackson, Mississippi 39225-3126

Estes Park Music (BMI)
2803 Bransford Ave.
Nashville, Tennessee 37204-3101

Evileria Music (BMI)
Address Unavailable

Exile Publishing Ltd.
Address Unavailable

Extraslick Music (ASCAP)
9001 8th Ave.
Inglewood, California 90305

Eye Cue Music (ASCAP)
see Wixen Music Publishing

F

Fame Brand Music (ASCAP)
see Universal-MCA Music Publishing

Famous Music (ASCAP)
1633 Broadway, 11th Fl.
New York, New York 10019

Fancy Footwork Music (ASCAP)
52 Meadow Ln.
Roslyn, New York 11577

Faust's Haus Music (BMI)
c/o King, Purtich, Holmes, et. al.
1900 Avenue of the Stars, Ste. 2500
Los Angeles, California 90067

FCG Music (ASCAP)
see EMI Music Publishing

Featherbed Music Inc. (BMI)
see Warner-Chappell Music

Ferry Hill Songs (ASCAP)
see Warner-Chappell Music

Bryan Ferry Publishing Designee (PRS)
Address Unavailable

Field Code Music (BMI)
2431 North Spaulding Ave.
Chicago, Illinois 60647

Fieldysnuttz Music (BMI)
Address Unavailable

Fingas Goal Music (ASCAP)
see EMI Music Publishing

FIPP International (BMI)
420 Jefferson Ave.
Miami Beach, Florida 33139

513 Music (BMI)
see Windswept Pacific Entertainment

Five Superstars (ASCAP)
see Almo Music

Fleck Music (BMI)
see Bug Music

List of Publishers

Flying Earform Music (BMI)
8935 Lindblade St.
Culver City, California 90023

FMK (ASCAP)
c/o Michael Curtis
130 Old Brompton Ln.
Killen, Alabama 35645

Fo Shawna Productions (ASCAP)
see Warner-Chappell Music

FOB Music Publishing (ASCAP)
825 Topsail Ln.
Secaucus, New Jersey 07094

444 Days (ASCAP)
240 Park Ave. South, Ste. 3
New York, New York 10003

Four Sons Music (ASCAP)
see Sony ATV Tunes LLC

Four Ya Ear Music
Address Unavailable

Fox Film Music (BMI)
P.O. Box 900, Bldg. 18
Beverly Hills, California 90213

Frankly Music (BMI)
8756 Holloway Dr.
Los Angeles, California 90069

Dwight Frye Music (BMI)
72 Madison Ave., 8th Fl.
New York, New York 10016

Fun With Goats Music (ASCAP)
see EMI Music Publishing

Funky Noble Productions (ASCAP)
see Warner-Chappell Music

Funzalo Music (BMI)
P.O. Box 35880
Tucson, Arizona 85740

Future Furniture (ASCAP)
see EMI Music Publishing

G

G Matt Music (ASCAP)
see Warner-Chappell Music

Gemarc (ASCAP)
see EMI Music Publishing

Generation 3rd Music (BMI)
see Notting Hill Music

Geto Boys and Girls Music (BMI)
c/o Bluewater Music Corp.
P.O. Box 120904
Nashville, Tennessee 37212

Ghetto Fabulous Entertainment (ASCAP)
105-84 Flatlands
10th St.
Brooklyn, New York 11236

Gimme Back My Publishing (ASCAP)
see Bug Music

Gintoe Music (BMI)
Address Unavailable

Glad Brad Music (ASCAP)
see Wixen Music Publishing

Glitterfish Music (BMI)
P.O. Box 50314
Nashville, Tennessee 37205

Gloria's Boy Music (ASCAP)
see EMI Music Publishing

Gnat Booty Music (ASCAP)
see Chrysalis Music

God Given Music (BMI)
2479 Peachtree Rd., Ste. 105
Atlanta, Georgia 30305

Godchildren Music (BMI)
see EMI Music Publishing

God's Crying Publishing (ASCAP)
see Sony ATV Tunes LLC

Gold and Iron Music Publishing (ASCAP)
see Warner-Chappell Music

Gottahaveable Music (BMI)
see Windswept Pacific Entertainment

GQ Romeo Music (BMI)
see Warner-Chappell Music

Grabbing Hands Music (ASCAP)
see EMI Music Publishing

Greenfund (ASCAP)
see Warner-Chappell Music

Greenhorse Music (BMI)
see EMI Music Publishing

Grindtime Publishing (BMI)
8015 South Yates
Chicago, Illinois 60617

Groobin Music (ASCAP)
see EMI Music Publishing

Ground Control Music (BMI)
see EMI Music Publishing

Grunge Girl Music (ASCAP)
see EMI Music Publishing

H

Hacklebarney Music (ASCAP)
426 Grant St.
Iowa City, Iowa 52240

Hale Yeah Music (SESAC)
see EMI Music Publishing

Halhana Music Publishing (ASCAP)
see Universal-MCA Music Publishing

Hand in My Pocket Music (ASCAP)
see Windswept Pacific Entertainment

Happy Ditties from Paradise (ASCAP)
see EMI Music Publishing

Hapsack Music (BMI)
see Copyright Management Services

Jamie Hawkins Publishers (BMI)
360 Grand Ave., No. 158
Oakland, California 94610

Headquarters Records
Address Unavailable

Hear Yie Music (ASCAP)
see Universal-MCA Music Publishing

Herbilicious Music (ASCAP)
see EMI Music Publishing

Hey Chubby Music (ASCAP)
see EMI Music Publishing

Hidden Scrolls Publishing (ASCAP)
244 Fifth Ave., Ste. Q269
New York, New York 10001

Hillabeans Music (ASCAP)
see Warner-Chappell Music

Hit & Run Music Publishing (ASCAP)
see EMI Music Publishing

Hitco Music (BMI)
see Windswept Pacific Entertainment

Hitco South (ASCAP)
see Windswept Pacific Entertainment

Hold Jack Music (BMI)
Address Unavailable

Hollow Thigh Music (BMI)
see Careers-BMG Music Publishing

Hot Cha Music (BMI)
c/o Gelfand, Rennert & Feldman
1301 Avenue of the Americas
10th Fl.
New York, New York 10019

Hot Heat Music (ASCAP)
see EMI Music Publishing

House of Cash (BMI)
see Bug Music

House of Fame (ASCAP)
P.O. Box 3629
Muscle Shoals, Alabama 35662

Melanie Howard Music (ASCAP)
1902 Wedgewood Ave.
Nashville, Tennessee 37212

List of Publishers

Howlin' Hits Music (ASCAP)
P.O. Box 163870
Austin, Texas 78716

Hunglikeyora (ASCAP)
see EMI Music Publishing

Huss Zwingli Publishing (ASCAP)
c/o DAS Communications
83 Riverside Dr.
New York, New York 10023

Hydroponic Music (BMI)
c/o Adam Raspler Management
946 N. Croft Ave.
Los Angeles, California 90069-4204

I

I Love the Punk Rock Music (BMI)
see Universal-MCA Music Publishing

I Want My Daddies Records (ASCAP)
see Warner-Chappell Music

Ice Trey Music (ASCAP)
see Big Red Tractor Music

Enrique Iglesias Music (ASCAP)
see EMI Music Publishing

Ill Will Music (ASCAP)
see Zomba Enterprises

I'm Nobody Music (ASCAP)
see Warner-Chappell Music

I'm With the Band Music (ASCAP)
see Warner-Chappell Music

In Love (ASCAP)
see Zomba Enterprises

Incense Productions (BMI)
c/o Fantasy Inc.
2600 Tenth St.
Berkeley, California 94710

Inky Sisi Music (BMI)
231 North 3rd St., Apt. 119
Philadelphia, Pennsylvania 19106

Innocent Bystander Music (ASCAP)
c/o VWC Management
13343 Bellevue Redmond Rd.
Ste. 201
Bellevue, Washington 98005

Interscope Music Publishing (ASCAP)
10900 Wilshire Blvd., Ste. 100
Los Angeles, California 90024

Irving Music (BMI)
2440 Sepulveda Blvd., Ste. 119
Los Angeles, California 90064

It Hurtz Music
Address Unavailable

It Was Written Publishing (ASCAP)
250 Maner Terr.
Smyrna, Georgia 30080

Ivy League Music
Address Unavailable

J

J Brasco (ASCAP)
P.O. Box 330-911
Brooklyn, New York 11233

Jackie Frost Music
Address Unavailable

Dylan Jackson Music (ASCAP)
see Warner-Chappell Music

Jade EG Music (BMI)
2440 Sepulveda Blvd., Ste. 119
Los Angeles, California 90064

Jagged Music (ASCAP)
see Warner-Chappell Music

Jahque Joints (SESAC)
see Universal-MCA Music Publishing

Jajapo Music (ASCAP)
see Universal-MCA Music Publishing

Jake and the Phatman Music (ASCAP)
c/o Glenn Standridge
19950 Santa Maria Ave., #E
Castro Valley, California 94546

Jasons Lyrics (SESAC)
12126 Killy Brook Dr.
Houston, Texas 77071-2725

Jat Cat Music Publishing (ASCAP)
see Universal-MCA Music Publishing

Jay Qui Music (ASCAP)
see EMI Music Publishing

Jessy Jaye Music (ASCAP)
128 Sprecher Ave.
Cleveland, Ohio 44130

Jelly's Jams LLC Music (ASCAP)
235 Park Avenue South, 10th Fl.
New York, New York 10003

Jerk Awake Music (ASCAP)
c/o Manatt Phelps & Phillips
11355 W. Olympic Blvd.
Los Angeles, California 90064

Rodney Jerkins Productions (BMI)
see EMI Music Publishing

Fred Jerkins Publishing (BMI)
see Famous Music

Jersey Girl Music (ASCAP)
see EMI Music Publishing

Jesus Never Fails Publishing (BMI)
c/o Heavenly Tunes Publishing
2476 West 251st St.
Lomita, California 90717

Jewel Music Publishing (ASCAP)
254 West 54th St., 13th Fl.
New York, New York 10019

Jobete Music (ASCAP)
see EMI Music Publishing

Jones Falls Music (BMI)
see EMI Music Publishing

Jones Music America (ASCAP)
c/o RZO
110 West 57th St., 7th Fl.
New York, New York 10019

Jordan Rocks Music (ASCAP)
see Warner-Chappell Music

JR Distribution Music (BMI)
see Sony ATV Tunes LLC

JuJu Rhythms (ASCAP)
see EMI Music Publishing

Jumping Bean Songs (BMI)
235 Park Ave. South, 10th Fl.
New York, New York 10003-1405

K

K Stuff Publishing (BMI)
120 East Hartsdale Ave., Apt. 3D
Hartsdale, New York 10530

Kandacy Music (ASCAP)
see EMI Music Publishing

Kander & Ebb (BMI)
see Warner-Chappell Music

Keepin It Real How Bout You Music (BMI)
see Warner-Chappell Music

R. Kelly Music (BMI)
see Zomba Songs

Kelodies (ASCAP)
see Warner-Chappell Music

Key Mark Music (BMI)
Address Unavailable

Key 2 My Heart Publishing (ASCAP)
2107 South Grand, Apt. 304
St. Louis, Missouri 63104

Killa Cam Music (ASCAP)
1339 Queen Anne Rd.
Teaneck, New Jersey 07666

List of Publishers

Killah Stealth Music (BMI)
1201 Barringer St.
Philadelphia, Pennsylvania 19119

Kissing Booth Music (BMI)
c/o Kramer Balabn Financial Service
12300 Wilshire Blvd., Ste. 300
Los Angeles, California 90025

Knoc Turn Al Music (BMI)
Address Unavailable

L

La Coriya's Songs (ASCAP)
c/o Lamenga, Kafi, Ford
563 Westminster Ave.
Elizabeth, New Jersey 07208

Labor Force Publishing (ASCAP)
312 Crosstown Rd., #103
Peachtree City, Georgia 30269

LaGamorph (ASCAP)
see Cherry Lane Music

Larga Vista Music (ASCAP)
c/o BPJ Administration
P.O. Box 218061
Nashville, Tennessee 37221

Largossa Music
Address Unavailable

Lastrada Music (ASCAP)
1344 Broadway, Ste. 208
Hewlett, New York 11557

LBV Songs (BMI)
c/o Ziffren, Brittenham et al.
1801 Century Park West
Los Angeles, California 90067

Lehsem Songs (BMI)
8756 Holloway Dr.
Los Angeles, California 90069

Lenono Music (BMI)
see EMI Music Publishing

Lexy's Daddy's Music (ASCAP)
15 Mountain Lakes Rd.
Oakland, New Jersey 07436

Libren Music (ASCAP)
c/o Provident Financial Mgmt.
10345 West Olympic Blvd., 2nd Fl.
Los Angeles, California 90064

Life Force Music (BMI)
c/o The Royalty Network
224 West 30th St., Ste. 1007
New York, New York 10001

Life of the Record Music (ASCAP)
P.O. Box 128288
Nashville, Tennessee 37212

Lil Lu Lu Publishing (BMI)
see EMI Music Publishing

Lillywilly Music (ASCAP)
see Warner-Chappell Music

Little Chatterbox Music (BMI)
308 NE 2nd St.
Smithville, Texas 78957

Little Engine Entertainment (ASCAP)
see BMG Songs

Little Idiot Music (BMI)
see Warner-Chappell Music

Little Mole Music (ASCAP)
c/o Lippman Entertainment
814 South Westgate Ave., #100
Los Angeles, California 90049

Living Under a Rock Music (ASCAP)
see Universal-MCA Music Publishing

Livingsting Music (ASCAP)
see Warner-Chappell Music

Loeffler Music (ASCAP)
see Warner-Chappell Music

Lone Talisman Music (ASCAP)
3245 Hamby Rd.
Alpharetta, Georgia 30004

Lonely Town Music (ASCAP)
11 Hardman Terr.
Denville, New Jersey 07834

Lonte Music (ASCAP)
see EMI Music Publishing

Loon Echo Music (BMI)
see Universal-MCA Music Publishing

Love N Loyalty Music (BMI)
c/o The Royalty Network
224 West 30th St., Ste. 1007
New York, New York 10001

Love Ranch Music (ASCAP)
see EMI Music Publishing

Lovely Sorts of Death Music (BMI)
P.O. Box 75995
Oklahoma City, Oklahoma 73147-1995

Lucky Girl Music (ASCAP)
28 East 92nd St., #1B
New York, New York 10128

Ludacris Music Publishing (ASCAP)
see EMI Music Publishing

M

M G III Music (ASCAP)
see EMI Music Publishing

Maanami Music (ASCAP)
see EMI Music Publishing

Magic Penny Music (ASCAP)
c/o MCS Music America, Inc.
1625 Broadway, 4th Fl.
Nashville, Tennessee 37203

Magnetic Publishing (PRS)
Address Unavailable

Major Bob Music (ASCAP)
1111 17th Ave. South
Nashville, Tennessee 37212

Make Shift Music (ASCAP)
1105 16th Ave. South, Ste. C
Nashville, Tennessee 37212

Maleahk Music (BMI)
P.O. Box 128112
Nashville, Tennessee 37212

Aimee Mann (ASCAP)
c/o Provident Financial Mgmt.
268 Newberry St., 4th Fl.
Boston, Massachusetts 02116

March Family Music (BMI)
30 Music Square West, Ste. 305
Nashville, Tennessee 37203

Marchninenth Music (ASCAP)
see Peermusic Ltd.

Marsky Music (BMI)
see EMI Music Publishing

Angie Martinez Music (ASCAP)
see EMI Music Publishing

Mas Venture Music (BMI)
2967 McCanless Rd.
Nolensville, Tennessee 37135

Mass Confusion Productions (ASCAP)
see Warner-Chappell Music

Christopher Matthew Music (BMI)
c/o Hitco Music Publishing
500 Bishop St., SW
Atlanta, Georgia 30318

Matzoh Ball Music (ASCAP)
see EMI Music Publishing

Mawga Dawg
Address Unavailable

Lyle Mays Music (BMI)
c/o Stevens and Company
76 Elm St., No. 304
Jamaica Plain, Massachusetts 02130-2800

Me and Chuma Music (ASCAP)
see EMI Music Publishing

Me and Marq Music (ASCAP)
see EMI Music Publishing

Me Three Publishing (BMI)
Address Unavailable

List of Publishers

Meeengya Music (ASCAP)
see Universal-MCA Music Publishing

Melee Savvy Music (BMI)
Address Unavailable

Melodious Fool Music (ASCAP)
see Warner-Chappell Music

Melusic Music (ASCAP)
see Warner-Chappell Music

Memphisto Music (ASCAP)
see Universal-MCA Music Publishing

Merchandyze Music (BMI)
see Warner-Chappell Music

Metrophonic Music
Address Unavailable

Jessica Michael Music (ASCAP)
see Warner-Chappell Music

Midtown Rock Music (ASCAP)
c/o Amp Management
3201 Cahuengia Blvd. W.
Los Angeles, California 90068

Mighty Moe Music (ASCAP)
c/o Jerome Earnest
P.O. Box 26158
Austin, Texas 78755

Mighty Nice Music (BMI)
c/o Bluewater Music Corp.
P.O. Box 120904
Nashville, Tennessee 37212

Migraine Music (ASCAP)
c/o Bill Annaruma
667 Carroll St.
Brooklyn, New York 11215

Mijac Music (BMI)
see Warner-Chappell Music

Mike City Music (BMI)
see Warner-Chappell Music

Mike Wrecka Music (ASCAP)
c/o The Royalty Network
224 West 30th St., Ste. 1007
New York, New York 10001

Milk Chocolate Factory (ASCAP)
see Sony ATV Tunes LLC

Milkbean Music (ASCAP)
240 Park Ave. South, Ste. 3
New York, New York 10003

Million Dollar Steve Music (BMI)
7955 SW 187th Terr.
Miami, Florida 33157

Mischkemusic (ASCAP)
see Windswept Pacific Entertainment

Miss Bessie Music (ASCAP)
c/o Provident Financial Mgmt.
10345 Olympic Blvd.
Los Angeles, California 90064

Misterssippi Music (BMI)
Address Unavailable

MJ Twelve Music (BMI)
see EMI Music Publishing

Mo Loving Music (ASCAP)
see Warner-Chappell Music

Moebetoblame Music (BMI)
c/o Myman et al.
11601 Wilshire Blvd., Ste. 200
Los Angeles, California 90025

Mofunk Music (ASCAP)
see Neutral Gray Music

Money Mack Music (BMI)
100 James Dr., Ste. 130
St. Rose, Louisiana 70087

Monkey C Music (BMI)
Address Unavailable

Mono Rat Music (ASCAP)
see EMI Music Publishing

More Sweeter Songs (ASCAP)
see Chrysalis Music

Morningside Trail Music (ASCAP)
see Peermusic Ltd.

Edwin H. Morris
see MPL Communications

Mortay Music Ltd.
Address Unavailable

Mosaic Music (BMI)
9200 Sunset Blvd., 10th Fl.
Los Angeles, California 90069

Mother Culture Publishing (ASCAP)
see Warner-Chappell Music

Mother Tracy Music (BMI)
c/o Gershorn Music Group
1908 Wedgewood Ave.
Nashville, Tennessee 37212

MPL Communications (ASCAP)
41 West 54th St.
New York, New York 10019

Mr. Bubba Music (BMI)
P.O. Box 888
Hermitage, Tennessee 37076

Mr. Cheeks Publishing (ASCAP)
see Universal-MCA Music Publishing

Mr. Manatti Music (BMI)
see EMI Music Publishing

Mr. Noise Music (BMI)
see Encore Entertainment LLC

Mr. Perry's Music Publishing (ASCAP)
312 Crosstown Rd., #103
Peachtree City, Georgia 30269

Mr. Spock Music (BMI)
see Warner-Chappell Music

Mr. Tan Man Music
Address Unavailable

Mrs. Lumpkin's Poodle (ASCAP)
see BMG Songs

MRX Music (ASCAP)
see Sony ATV Tunes LLC

Ms. Mary's Music (BMI)
see Warner-Chappell Music

Mudvayne Music (ASCAP)
see Zomba Enterprises

Murrah Music (BMI)
1109 16th Ave. South
Nashville, Tennessee 37212-2304

Mushroom Music (ASCAP)
Address Unavailable

Music That Music (ASCAP)
see EMI Music Publishing

Music in Three (BMI)
Address Unavailable

Music of Windswept (ASCAP)
see Windswept Pacific Entertainment

Musik Munk Publishing (BMI)
Address Unavailable

My Blue Car Music (ASCAP)
see Warner-Chappell Music

My Own Chit Publishing (BMI)
see EMI Music Publishing

My So Called Music (ASCAP)
c/o Flood et al.
5141 Virginia Way, #460
Brentwood, Tennessee 37027

Mytrell Publishing (BMI)
55 Crutchfield Dr.
Newport News, Virginia 23602

N

N Key Music (BMI)
see EMI Music Publishing

N The Water Publishing (ASCAP)
P.O. Box 924190
Houston, Texas 77292

Naked Under My Clothes Music (ASCAP)
see Chrysalis Music

List of Publishers

Nappy Roots Publishing (BMI)
Address Unavailable

Nasty Cat Music (BMI)
c/o Carol Vincent and Associates
P.O. Box 150657
Nashville, Tennessee 37215

Nate Dogg Music (BMI)
see Sony ATV Music

National League Music (BMI)
5455 Wilshire Blvd., Ste. 700
Los Angeles, California 90036

Natural Light Music (BMI)
Address Unavailable

Nedotykomka (ASCAP)
see Bug Music

Nelstar Publishing (SOCAN)
Address Unavailable

Henry Neuman Songs (BMI)
P.O. Box 684651
Austin, Texas 78768-4651

Neutral Gray Music (ASCAP)
405 W. 45th St., No. 4D
New York, New York 10036

New Columbia Pictures Music (ASCAP)
see Sony ATV Tunes LLC

New Hidden Valley Music (ASCAP)
see Warner-Chappell Music

Next Level Groove Music (ASCAP)
c/o Spirit Two Music Inc.
137 Fifth Ave., 8th Fl.
New York, New York 10010

Ninth Street Tunnel Music (BMI)
see Sony ATV Tunes LLC

Nipple Music (BMI)
100 West 57th St.
New York, New York 10019

Nippy Music (ASCAP)
60 Park Place, Ste. 1801
Newark, New Jersey 07102

Nivrac Tyke Music (ASCAP)
see EMI Music Publishing

NMG Music (ASCAP)
see EMI Music Publishing

No Good But So Good Music (BMI)
1166 NW 113th Terr.
Miami, Florida 33168

No Gravity Music (ASCAP)
see EMI Music Publishing

No KO Music (ASCAP)
see Bug Music

Noclist Music (ASCAP)
12 Revere Place
Newark, Delaware 19702

Noontime South (SESAC)
see Warner-Chappell Music

North Avenue Music (ASCAP)
see EMI Music Publishing

Nouveaux Music (BMI)
see Sony ATV Tunes LLC

Nuez Music (BMI)
19955 Briarcliff
Detroit, Michigan 48221

Nuyorican Publishing (BMI)
see Sony ATV Tunes LLC

NY O'Dae Music (BMI)
105-32 Flatlands
1st St.
Brooklyn, New York 11236

O

Obo Itself (ASCAP)
see Almo/Irving

Obverse Creation Music (ASCAP)
see Sony ATV Music

Old Crow Music (BMI)
see Warner-Chappell Music

One CRC Publishing (BMI)
4821 South Highway 27, Ste. B
Somerset, Kentucky 42501

139 7 Lenox Entertainment (ASCAP)
129 West 142nd St., Apt. 513
New York, New York 10030

1000 Lights Music Ltd.
Address Unavailable

1974 Music (ASCAP)
see Universal-MCA Music Publishing

Open Secret Music (ASCAP)
13045 W. Olympic Blvd.
Los Angeles, California 90064

Organized Noize Music (BMI)
see Windswept Pacific Entertainment

Original JB Music (ASCAP)
405 West 45th St., Ste. 4D
New York, New York 10036

Fernando Osorio Songs (BMI)
763 Couins Ave., Ste. 301
Miami Beach, Florida 33139

Ostaf Songs (BMI)
P.O. Box 91296
Los Angeles, California 90009

Our Trinity Music
Address Unavailable

Owl Rat Publishing (ASCAP)
c/o James Taylor
360 Hamilton Ave., Ste. 100
White Plains, New York 10601

P

Paniro's Publishing (ASCAP)
see EMI Music Publishing

Pastor Troy (BMI)
Address Unavailable

Pat Meth Music (BMI)
c/o Ted Kurland Associates
173 Brighton Ave.
Boston, Massachusetts 02134-2003

Pay Town Publishing (BMI)
1623 Berwick Ct.
Flossmoore, Illinois 60422

Peer International Corp. (BMI)
see Peermusic

Peermusic (BMI)
810 7th Ave.
New York, New York 10019-5818

Peermusic III (BMI)
see Peermusic Ltd.

Peermusic Ltd. (BMI)
5358 Melrose Blvd., Ste. 400
Los Angeles, California 90038

Peertunes LTD (SESAC)
see EMI Music Publishing

Pentagon Lipservices Real World (BMI)
see Hit & Run Music Publishing

Period Music
see Zomba Songs

Pez Music (BMI)
420 E. 72nd St., #20B
New York, New York 10021

Phat Nasty Publishing (BMI)
2508 N. Pace Blvd.
Pensacola, Florida 32505

Pigfoot Music (ASCAP)
c/o The Royalty Network
418 B Street, Ste. 400
New York, New York 10025

Pimp Yug (ASCAP)
see Warner-Chappell Music

Pink Panther Music (ASCAP)
see EMI Music Publishing

Elsie Louise Pitts Music (BMI)
see Universal-MCA Music Publishing

List of Publishers

Pladis Music (ASCAP)
see EMI Music Publishing

Platinum Plow (ASCAP)
see Warner-Chappell Music

Po Ho Productions (ASCAP)
see Universal-MCA Music Publishing

Polygram International Publishing (ASCAP)
see Universal-MCA Music Publishing

Polypterus Music (BMI)
see Warner-Chappell Music

Pookietoots Publishing (ASCAP)
see Universal-MCA Music Publishing

Pop Rox Music (ASCAP)
see Cherry Lane Music

Post Oak Publishing (BMI)
c/o Friedman and La Rosa
747 3rd Ave.
New York, New York 10017

Potty Mouth Publishing (BMI)
see Warner-Chappell Music

Protoons (ASCAP)
P.O. Box 388
Holbrook, New Jersey 11741

Q

Q Baby Music (ASCAP)
Address Unavailable

Quartet Music (ASCAP)
c/o Leiber & Stoller
9000 Sunset Blvd., Ste. 1107
Los Angeles, California 90069

R

R and Bling Music (ASCAP)
76 Palisade Ave.
White Plains, New York 10607

Rainbow Fish Publishing (BMI)
Address Unavailable

Ramshackle Music
Address Unavailable

Denny Randell Music (BMI)
340 South Farrell Dr., Ste. A-112
Palm Springs, California 92262-7921

Range Road Music (ASCAP)
c/o Carlin America, Inc.
126 East 38th St.
New York, New York 10016

Rat Eater Music (BMI)
2608 Pioneer Trail, Apt. 807
Sandusky, Ohio 44870-5143

Ray Farm Music (BMI)
see Bug Music

Razmataz Songs
Address Unavailable

Reach Global Songs (BMI)
see Reach Music International

Reach Music International (ASCAP)
217 E. 86th St., Ste. 117
New York, New York 10028

Real World Music (PRS)
Address Unavailable

Realsongs (ASCAP)
6363 Sunset Blvd., Ste. 810
Hollywood, California 90028

Restaurant's World Music (ASCAP)
807 Lockwood
Royal Oak, Michigan 48067

Revolutionary Jazz Giant (BMI)
c/o Wilson and Associates
10474 Santa Monica, No. 304
Los Angeles, California 90025

Riddum Music (BMI)
see Sony ATV Tunes LLC

Ripplestick Music (BMI)
Address Unavailable

Rive Droite Music (BMI)
22761 Pacific Coast Hwy., Ste. 227
Malibu, California 90265

Rocks LLC (ASCAP)
159 West 25th St., 4th Fl.
New York, New York 10001

Ron G Music (BMI)
see EMI Music Publishing

Rondo Music London (PRS)
Address Unavailable

Rosasharn Music (BMI)
Address Unavailable

Round Tower Publishing
Address Unavailable

Rush Groove Records (ASCAP)
see Protoons

Marc Russel Songs (ASCAP)
c/o Make It Rock Productions
7 Pratt Blvd.
Glen Cove, New York 11542

Rutland Road Music (ASCAP)
see Warner-Chappell Music

Rykomusic (ASCAP)
101 Charles Drive, Bldg. #1
Bryn Mawr, Pennsylvania 19010

S

Sababa G (ASCAP)
c/o Guy Erez
608 S. Burnside Ave., #1
Los Angeles, California 90036

Saja Music Co. (BMI)
see Lastrada Music

Sanga Music (BMI)
250 W. 57th St., Ste. 1218
New York, New York 10107

Sarangel Music (ASCAP)
see Bug Music

Satisfaction Fulfilled Ltd. (PRS)
Address Unavailable

Scribble Ink Publishing (ASCAP)
c/o IDRS Mills
P.O. Box 24154
Cincinnati, Ohio 45224

Sea Gayle Music (ASCAP)
see EMI Music Publishing

Sedge Music (ASCAP)
see Cherry Lane Music

Seether Publishing (BMI)
72 Madison Ave., 8th Fl.
New York, New York 10016

Senseless Music (BMI)
see Universal-MCA Music Publishing

Serrano 105 Publishing (ASCAP)
c/o Eartha V. Moore
10581 National Blvd.
Los Angeles, California 90034

757 Music (ASCAP)
c/o Garland W. Mosley Jr.
514 Willowgreen Ct.
Chesapeake, Virginia 23320

Sevens International (ASCAP)
23 Music Square East, #400
Nashville, Tennessee 37201

Shack Suga Entertainment (ASCAP)
see EMI Music Publishing

Shane Minor Music (BMI)
see EMI Music Publishing

Shannon River Music (BMI)
see Windswept Pacific Entertainment

Sharay's Music (ASCAP)
see Warner-Chappell Music

Damon Sharpe Music (ASCAP)
see Warner-Chappell Music

She Writes Her Own Music (ASCAP)
269 West Walnut Lane, #1R
Philadelphia, Pennsylvania 19144

List of Publishers

Shellayla Songs (BMI)
Address Unavailable

Shelly's House Music
Address Unavailable

Sherlock Holmes Music Ltd.
Address Unavailable

Sick Muse Songs
see EMI Music Publishing

Silver Fiddle Music (ASCAP)
see Wixen Music Publishing

Paul Simon Music (BMI)
1619 Broadway, Ste. 500
New York, New York 10019-7412

Singletrack Music (BMI)
see Windswept Pacific Entertainment

Sir George Music (ASCAP)
see Warner-Chappell Music

600 Foot Hedgehog Music (ASCAP)
c/o James B. Wood
P.O. Box 1033
Summerland, California 93067

SKG Music Publishing (ASCAP)
see Cherry Lane Music

Skizzneck Music (ASCAP)
c/o Nick Ben-Meir
652 North Doheny Dr.
Los Angeles, California 90064

Slavery Music (BMI)
see Universal-MCA Music Publishing

E. O. Smith Music (BMI)
see Wixen Music Publishing

Richard Smith Publishing (ASCAP)
5 Linden St., Apt. 4H
Hackensack, New Jersey 07601

Smoobie Music (ASCAP)
217 High St.
Sharon Hill, Pennsylvania 19079

Smooth C Publishing (BMI)
see Windswept Pacific Entertainment

Sniff It Music (ASCAP)
see EMI Music Publishing

So So Def Music (ASCAP)
see EMI Music Publishing

Soldierz Touch (ASCAP)
see Famous Music

Sometimes You Win Music (ASCAP)
see Chrysalis Music

Song Auction Music (ASCAP)
759 Bresslyn Rd.
Nashville, Tennessee 37205

Song of Cash (ASCAP)
see Bug Music

Song Paddock Music (ASCAP)
c/o T.K. Kimbrell
P.O. Box 440090
Nashville, Tennessee 37244

Songs of API (BMI)
Address Unavailable

Songs of Dreamworks (BMI)
see Cherry River Music

Songs of Lastrada (BMI)
see Lastrada Music

Songs of Mosaic (ASCAP)
c/o Lionel Conway
9200 Sunset Blvd.
Los Angeles, California 90069

Songs of Nashville Dreamworks (BMI)
see Cherry River Music

Songs of Otis Barker (ASCAP)
see Howlin' Hits Music

Songs of Peer (ASCAP)
5358 Melrose Ave., Ste. 400
Los Angeles, California 90039

Songs of Teracel (BMI)
see Sony ATV Tunes LLC

Songs of Universal (BMI)
see Universal-MCA Music Publishing

Songs of Windswept Pacific (BMI)
see Windswept Pacific Entertainment

Songwriters Paddock Music (BMI)
1107 17th Ave. South
Nashville, Tennessee 37212

Sonic Grafitti (ASCAP)
see EMI Music Publishing

Sonik Tooth Music (BMI)
see Zomba Songs

Sonotrock Music (BMI)
108 Fourth Ave. South, #207
Franklin, Tennessee 37064

Sony/ATV Acuff Rose Music (BMI)
see Sony ATV Tunes LLC

Sony/ATV Latin Music Publishing (BMI)
605 Lincoln Rd., Ste. 303
Miami Beach, Florida 33139

Sony ATV Music (ASCAP)
550 Madison Ave.
New York, New York 10022

Sony ATV Songs LLC (BMI)
8 Music Square West
Nashville, Tennessee 37203

Sony ATV Tree Publishing (BMI)
see Sony ATV Tunes LLC

Sony ATV Tunes LLC (ASCAP)
8 Music Square West
Nashville, Tennessee 37203

Sony Tunes (ASCAP)
see Sony ATV Music

Soul Child Music (ASCAP)
see Universal-MCA Music Publishing

Souljah Music (ASCAP)
see Famous Music

Southern Boy Publishing
Address Unavailable

Southern Melody Publishing
P.O. Box 55300
Durham, North Carolina 27717-5300

Sparkling Beatnik Music
Address Unavailable

Special Rider Music (SESAC)
P.O. Box 860
New York, New York 10276-0860

Specific Harm Music (ASCAP)
see Sony ATV Tunes LLC

Spread Your Cheeks (ASCAP)
see Warner-Chappell Music

Bruce Springsteen Publishing (ASCAP)
c/o Jon Landau Management, Inc.
80 Mason St.
Greenwich, Connecticut 06830

Spunkersongs (ASCAP)
see Universal-MCA Music Publishing

Spydox Publishing (BMI)
240 Wortman Ave., Apt. 7A
Brooklyn, New York 11207

Squint Songs (ASCAP)
see Acuff Rose Music Publishing

Stairway to Bittner's Music (BMI)
see Windswept Pacific Entertainment

Stereo Supersonic Music (ASCAP)
1187 Coast Village Rd., Ste. #1
Montecito, California 93108

Ray Stevens Music (BMI)
1707 Grand Ave.
Nashville, Tennessee 37212

Still N The Water Publishing (BMI)
see Warner-Chappell Music

Stone Agate Music (BMI)
see EMI Music Publishing

Stone City Music (ASCAP)
see National League Music

List of Publishers

Stone Diamond Music (BMI)
see EMI Music Publishing

Strange Beautiful Music (ASCAP)
c/o Siegel, Feldstein & Doffin
2020 Union St.
San Francisco, California 94123

Strange Motel Music (ASCAP)
c/o Platinum Gold Music
18653 Ventura Blvd., Ste. 292
Tarzana, California 91356

Stratosphericyoness Music (BMI)
Address Unavailable

Strictly TQ Music (ASCAP)
see Sony ATV Tunes LLC

The Strokes Band Music (ASCAP)
c/o Mr. Victor Wlodinguer, CPA
15 East 26th St., #1803
New York, New York 10010

Strongsongs Ltd.
Address Unavailable

Stuck in the Throat (ASCAP)
see Famous Music

Stygian Songs (ASCAP)
see Wixen Music Publishing

Sufferin Succotash Songs (ASCAP)
see Zomba Enterprises

Suge Publishing (ASCAP)
see Warner-Chappell Music

Suite Twelve O Two Music (BMI)
see Tommy Boy Music

Sunny Vista Music (BMI)
see Bug Music

Superhype Publishing (ASCAP)
see Warner-Chappell Music

Supreme Lee Music
Address Unavailable

Swallow Turn Music (ASCAP)
see Wixen Music Publishing

Sweet River Music (ASCAP)
c/o Ampex Corp.
401 Broadway, M.S. 3-36
Redwood City, California 94063-3126

Swing T Publishing (BMI)
9435 M Washington Blvd., Ste. A
Laurel, Maryland 20723

Swinstone (ASCAP)
c/o Emerson Swinford
802 Ogden Dr.
Los Angeles, California 90036

T

T H I O (ASCAP)
14351 Hortense St.
Sherman Oaks, California 91423

T-Lev Music
Address Unavailable

Tabulous Music (ASCAP)
see Windswept Pacific Entertainment

TCF Music Publishing (ASCAP)
see Twentieth Century-Fox Music Corp.

Te Bass Music (BMI)
see EMI Music Publishing

Teamsta Entertainment Music (BMI)
c/o The Royalty Network
224 West 30th St., Ste. 1007
New York, New York 10001

Tear It Down Music (ASCAP)
see EMI Music Publishing

Temporary Music (BMI)
see Warner-Chappell Music

Ten Ten Tunes (ASCAP)
33 Music Square West, Ste. 110
Nashville, Tennessee 37203

Tennessee Colonel (ASCAP)
c/o Addington Fields, Mgmt.
1719 West End Ave.
East Tower, Ste. 614
Nashville, Tennessee 37203

Tennessee Hills Music (BMI)
c/o Tree Publishing Co.
P.O. Box 1273
Nashville, Tennessee 37202

Tennman Tunes (ASCAP)
see Zomba Enterprises

Teracel Music (ASCAP)
see Sony ATV Tunes LLC

Terrardome Music (ASCAP)
see EMI Music Publishing

Testatyme Music (ASCAP)
see Almo Music

Tetragrammaton Music (ASCAP)
see Universal-MCA Music Publishing

Them Damn Twins Music (ASCAP)
see EMI Music Publishing

The Thick Plottens Music (ASCAP)
see Warner-Chappell Music

Third Palm Music (BMI)
c/o Cohen and Cohen
740 North La Brea Ave., 2nd Fl.
Los Angeles, California 90038-3339

Thirty Two Mile Music (BMI)
see Warner-Chappell Music

THM Music (BMI)
see Bug Music

Tiarra's Daddy Music (BMI)
see Universal-MCA Music Publishing

Cori Tiffani Publishing (BMI)
see Sony ATV Tunes LLC

Tokeco Tunes (BMI)
1107 17th Ave. South
Nashville, Tennessee 37212

Tommy Boy Music (BMI)
902 Broadway, 13th Fl.
New York, New York 10010

Alvin Toney Music (ASCAP)
c/o Serling, Rooks, & Ferrara
254 West 54th St., 14th Fl.
New York, New York 10019

Tony Toni Tone Music (ASCAP)
see Universal-MCA Music Publishing

Tornado Temple Music (BMI)
c/o Fitzgerald-Hartley Co.
34 N. Palm Ave.
Ventura, California 93001

Touched by Jazz Music (ASCAP)
see EMI Music Publishing

Traptism (SESAC)
see Warner-Chappell Music

Tremonti Stapp Music (BMI)
see Dwight Frye Music

Treyball Music (ASCAP)
c/o Gelfand, Rennert & Feldman
1880 Century Park East, Ste. 1600
Los Angeles, California 90067

Tri Angels Music (ASCAP)
see EMI Music Publishing

TTARP Music Publishing (BMI)
see Windswept Pacific Entertainment

Tuff Huff Music (BMI)
see Zomba Songs

Tunesmith Advancements (ASCAP)
see Sony ATV Tunes LLC

Turkey On Rye Music (ASCAP)
c/o Nick Ben-Meir, CPA
652 North Doheny Dr.
Los Angeles, California 90069

Turtle Wins the Race (ASCAP)
see Warner-Chappell Music

List of Publishers

TVT Music (ASCAP)
    23 E. 4th St.
    New York, New York 10003

Twentieth Century-Fox Music Corp. (ASCAP)
    P.O. Box 900
    Music Dept., Bldg. #18
    Beverly Hills, California 90213

21:1 Music
    Address Unavailable

Two Bagger Music (BMI)
    Address Unavailable

Two Roads Music (BMI)
    see Bug Music

2855 Music (ASCAP)
    500-425 Carrall St.
    Vancouver, British Columbia V6B 6E3
    Canada

Tziah Music (BMI)
    see Warner-Chappell Music

U

Ugmoe Music (ASCAP)
    see Universal-MCA Music Publishing

Uh Oh Entertainment (ASCAP)
    c/o Wlodinger, Erk, & Chanzis
    15 East 26th St., Ste. 1803
    New York, New York 10010

Un Rivera Publishing (BMI)
    see Untertainment Records

Uncle Bobby Music (BMI)
    see EMI Music Publishing

Uncle Hadley Music (ASCAP)
    1219 16th Ave. South
    Nashville, Tennessee 37212

Unichappell Music Inc. (BMI)
    see Warner-Chappell Music

Unitunes Music (ASCAP)
    c/o Anna Spano
    57-B Hymus Blvd.
    Pointe Claire, Quebec H9R 4T2
    Canada

Universal Duchess Music (BMI)
    see Universal-MCA Music Publishing

Universal MCA Music Ltd.
    Address Unavailable

Universal-MCA Music Publishing (ASCAP)
    2440 Sepulveda Blvd., Ste. 100
    Los Angeles, California 90064-1712

Universal Music Publishing (ASCAP)
    see Universal-MCA Music Publishing

Universal Music Publishing Int. Ltd.
    Address Unavailable

Universal Polygram International Pub.
    (ASCAP)
    see Universal-MCA Music Publishing

Universal-Polygram International Tunes
    (SESAC)
    99440 Collection Center Dr.
    Chicago, Illinois 60693-0994

Universal Songs of Polygram Intntl. (BMI)
    see Universal-MCA Music Publishing

Universal Tunes (SESAC)
    99440 Collection Center Dr.
    Chicago, Illinois 60693-0994

Untertainment Records (ASCAP)
    3 East 28th St., 9th Fl.
    New York, New York 10016

Unwritten Music (ASCAP)
    see Warner-Chappell Music

V

Phil Vassar Music (ASCAP)
    see EMI Music Publishing

Velvet Apple Music (BMI)
   1880 Century Park East, Ste. 1600
   Los Angeles, California 90067

Vice Game Music (BMI)
   see EMI Music Publishing

Virginia Beach Music (ASCAP)
   see Warner-Chappell Music

Viva La Cucaracha Music (ASCAP)
   see Cherry Lane Music

W

W B M Music (SESAC)
   see Warner-Chappell Music

Wait No More Music (BMI)
   c/o FBMM
   P.O. Box 331549
   Nashville, Tennessee 37203

Waltz Time Music (ASCAP)
   see EMI Music Publishing

Wangout
   Address Unavailable

Wannabite Music (ASCAP)
   see BMG Songs

Warner-Chappell Music (ASCAP)
   10585 Santa Monica Blvd.
   Los Angeles, California 90025

Warner/Chappell Music Ltd. (PRS)
   Address Unavailable

Warner-Tamerlane Publishing (BMI)
   see Warner-Chappell Music

Waters of Nazareth Publishing (BMI)
   see EMI Music Publishing

WB Music (ASCAP)
   see Warner-Chappell Music

Webo Girl Publishing (ASCAP)
   see Warner-Chappell Music

Weightless Cargo Music (BMI)
   1001 Caldwell Ave.
   Nashville, Tennessee 37204

Wells Music
   c/o The Songwriters Guild
   1500 Harbor Blvd.
   Weehawken, New Jersey 07087

Welsh Witch Music (BMI)
   see Sony ATV Tunes LLC

Wenonga Music (BMI)
   see Sony ATV Tunes LLC

Whalumusic (ASCAP)
   10345 West Olympic Blvd.
   Los Angeles, California 90064

White Pearl Songs (BMI)
   see Sony ATV Tunes LLC

White Rhino Music (BMI)
   23 East 4th St., 3rd Fl.
   New York, New York 10003-7023

Who Is She Music (BMI)
   c/o Burton Goldstein & Co.
   156 West 56th St., Ste. 1803
   New York, New York 10019-3800

Whorga Musica (ASCAP)
   see EMI Music Publishing

Wiener Art (ASCAP)
   see Peermusic Ltd.

Wigged Music (BMI)
   c/o Provident Financial Management
   10345 Olympic Blvd.
   Los Angeles, California 90064

Wiggly Tooth Music (ASCAP)
   see Warner-Chappell Music

Will Decide Ltd.
   Address Unavailable

Jerry Williams Music (BMI)
   see Bug Music

List of Publishers

Windswept Pacific Entertainment (ASCAP)
9320 Wiltshire Blvd., Ste. 200
Beverly Hills, California 90212-3217

Without Anna Music (ASCAP)
c/o Stokes et al.
901 18th Ave. South
Nashville, Tennessee 37212

Wixen Music Publishing (BMI)
24025 Park Sorrento, Ste. 130
Calabasas, California 91302-4003

Wonderland Music (BMI)
see Disney Music Publishing

Wonposet Songs (BMI)
725 4th Ave., #5KK
Brooklyn, New York 11232

Woolly Puddin' Music (BMI)
c/o Neil Hagaman PLLC
1025 16th Ave. South, Ste. 202
Nashville, Tennessee 37212

Words Ampersand Music (BMI)
c/o Tony Margherita Management
4040 N. Kedzie, 3rd Fl.
Chicago, Illinois 60618

World of the Dolphin Music (ASCAP)
see Universal-MCA Music Publishing

Worldwide West Music
Address Unavailable

Wretched Music (ASCAP)
see Warner-Chappell Music

Wu Shu Boy Music
Address Unavailable

X

Xtina Music (BMI)
see Careers-BMG Music Publishing

Y

Yellowbrick Road Music (ASCAP)
c/o Quincy Jones Music
3800 Barham Blvd., #503
Los Angeles, California 90068

Yezzimuzic
Address Unavailable

Yo Cats Music (BMI)
Address Unavailable

Young Crow Music (BMI)
Address Unavailable

Young Dude Music (ASCAP)
see Universal-MCA Music Publishing

Your Mother's Music (BMI)
c/o Eric T. Sadler
1872 Hickory Ln.
Atlantic Beach, Florida 32233

Z

Z Bo and Happy Publishing (BMI)
99 NW 183rd St., Ste. 201
Miami, Florida 33169

Zarathustra Music (ASCAP)
c/o Elliot Goldenthal
874 Broadway, Apt. 1001
New York, New York 10003

Zevon Music (BMI)
1880 Century Park East, Ste. 1600
Los Angeles, California 90067

Zomba Enterprises (ASCAP)
138 West 25th St., 8th Fl.
New York, New York 10001

Zomba Songs (BMI)
137-139 West 25th St.
New York, New York 10001-7200